D0096370

PRAISE FOR *THE POWER OF 1440*

"If it feels like your days are slipping through your fingers, *The Power of 1440* is the key to seizing your opportunities. By empowering you to recognize just how important a single day can be, my friend Tim gives you practical tools to maximize your one and only life, one moment at a time."

—Steven Furtick
Pastor of Elevation Church and *New York Times* bestselling author

"Like a cool breeze on a hot day, *The Power of 1440* offers a breath of fresh air for us on our daily journey. Tim Timberlake cuts through the accumulation of obligations and expectations crowding our schedules and helps us see the incredible gift of time we're given each day. As practical as it is profound, this book is sure to be savored by anyone wanting to simplify their life and deepen their faith. Highly recommended!"

—Chris Hodges
Senior pastor of Church of the Highlands and author of *The Daniel Dilemma* and *Out of the Cave*

"When it comes to loving life, Tim Timberlake lives what he preaches, and his enthusiasm and passion are an inspiration to everyone around him. He truly understands how to make each minute and each moment count. I've always admired that about him, which is why I'm happy he has distilled his life philosophy into his newest book, *The Power of 1440*. If you've ever been held back by the failures of yesterday or intimidated by the unknowns of tomorrow (and who among us hasn't?), then *The Power of 1440* will help you make the most of the only thing you can really control: today. Tim truly understands how to make each moment count."

—Judah Smith
Lead pastor of Churchome

"Tim Timberlake is truly one of the most creative minds on the planet. His new book shows us the power and value of time. After reading this book, you will never view a day the same way. His imagination and faith challenge us to think about what can happen in just one minute of any day. This book is a must read for all of us who are blessed with amazing minutes every day."

—Tim Storey
Speaker and life coach

"It can be easy to be focused on so many different things that we miss out on the simple truth that each of us has the same amount of time each day. Regardless of our current circumstance, what we're praying for, or what we're working toward, we each have the same 1440 minutes in a day. Tim's encouragement to be thankful for the time we have, and also to be intentional in everything we do, are words that will help us live a life that's more joyful, more impactful, and ultimately closer to God and His will for our lives."

—Chad Veach
Lead pastor of Zoe Church LA

"Tim Timberlake is so many things. Pastor, leader, husband, father, writer, and I have the joy of calling him friend. Tim is one of my favorite communicators and a regularly featured guest speaker at Sandals Church. Tim is also an incredible thinker and writer. In *The Power of 1440*, Tim will challenge you to take advantage of the same gift God has given all of us: the gift of time. I have personally watched Tim make the most of his time, and this book will help you to make the most of yours. Don't waste another minute! Pick up this book today, and step in the destiny God has waiting for you. *The Power of 1440* will help you get there. The clock is ticking!"

—Matt Brown
Pastor of Sandals Church and author of *A Book Called YOU*

"Tim is an incredible husband, pastor, and friend—a servant leader and phenomenal man of God. I am convinced that this book, *The Power of 1440*, will empower and inspire you to utilize every minute of every day to become all that God has destined you to be!"

—Earl McClellan
Senior pastor of Shoreline City Church

"I am so excited for the world to get their hands on *The Power of 1440*. In this book, Tim Timberlake so beautifully reminds us of the power of each minute that God has given us. In the times that we are living in, it's so easy to fill our days with complaints of worry and boredom, but Tim gives us the beautiful reminder that we are charged each moment with fulfilling the purpose God has given us here on earth. I have known Tim for years, and when I read *The Power of 1440*, I knew it was something special that everyone needs to get their hands on. This book is a powerful reminder of the value of how we spend each day."

—Chris Durso
Author of *The Heist and Misfit* and
pastor of Saints Church

"I have so much respect and love for Pastor Tim. His heart is made of pure gold, his passion for people inspires me, and his friendship is one I cherish deeply. *The Power of 1440* is such a profound yet simple message with the power to reshape our perspectives and thus change our lives and the lives of those around us. This book is like looking at life with the fresh lenses we all need—and it sure makes a world of a difference."

—Dino Rizzo
Executive director of Association
of Related Churches (ARC)

"One of the things I love most about Tim is his passion. But what I love even more is that he carries a depth that only comes from a deeply rooted commitment to God and His Word. When Tim communicates, it's powerful—it will make you think. But it's also practical—it calls you to action, because that's where the change comes. *The Power of 1440* is an essential read for anyone looking to make the most out of their life. The principles within are timeless truths that are foundational for every person who wants to fulfill their calling and maximize their impact on the world around them."

—John Siebeling
Pastor of The Life Church

"Over the course of my career as a professor I've encountered many overwhelmed students. I made a point of sharing my own story with them. I worked my way through college, seminary, and graduate school. Fifteen of those years meant working full time, providing for my wife and children, and serving in the local church while being a full-time student. I didn't know it at the time, but I was prepared for that future by something a professor told me as a freshman in college: 'Five minutes is a long time.' I never forgot it, and frequently applied it. That simple sentence changed my life. Tim Timberlake's book teaches readers the same crucial lesson. We have more than five minutes a day to manage the tasks set before us by a loving God who built us to handle stress. We have 1440 of them. What we need to do is steward them wisely, not matter what our tasks and circumstances. The Lord will do the rest."

—Dr. Michael S. Heiser
Executive director of the Awakening School of Theology and Ministry, bestselling author, and host of the *Naked Bible Podcast*

"Too often we wake up and our first thought is, *I've just got to get through today*. But life was meant to be a joy, not a slog. My friend Tim's book is a much-needed reminder that every day (and every single minute) is a precious gift, given equally to every one of us. Read this book, and change that first thought each morning to, *This day is going to be amazing*."

—Greg Surratt
Founding pastor of Seacoast Church and president of Association of Related Churches (ARC)

"Tim Timberlake invites us to leverage every moment we are given to the glory of God and toward an abundant, flourishing life. This book is not just a theory or theology; this is how he actually lives his life. If you want best practices on abundant living from someone who practices an abundant life, read this book."

—Stovall and Kerri Weems
Founders and global senior pastors of Celebration Church and authors of books including *The God-First Life* and *Rhythms of Grace*

"I've always liked Tim Timberlake and am honored to call him my friend. Any amount of time you spend with him will leave you deeper in the Word, challenged to press in, and encouraged to press on. And *The Power of 1440* will not disappoint, with practically written guidance for everyone to implement every day. Tim brilliantly helps us step through how to walk out apostle Paul's challenge in Ephesians 4:15–16, to 'be very careful, then, how you live—not as unwise but as wise, making the most of every opportunity, because the days are evil.' If you want to learn how to make the most of *every* opportunity, this book is for you."

—Rick Bezet
Lead pastor of New Life Church of Arkansas
and author of *Be Real* and *Real Love*

"*The Power of 1440* is a powerful encouragement to everyone, no matter your age or story. Tim Timberlake's passion to live in the moment and maximize the present is contagious through every page. His practical approach to the power of each day will empower you to step into all that God has prepared for your life. His love for Jesus and others is evident through his life and the pages of this incredible book."

—Rich Wilkerson Jr.
Lead pastor of VOUS Church and author of
Sandcastle Kings and *Friend of Sinners*

"It has been said that one of God's greatest gifts to us is time. However, what we do with it is our gift to him. In this timely, tactful, and necessary work, Tim Timberlake gives us kingdom keys to wisely steward our time in ways that help us accomplish our purpose and at the same time protect our peace."

—Dharius Daniels
Lead pastor of Change Church and author of *RePresent*
Jesus and Relational Intelligence: The People Skills
You Need for the Life of Purpose You Want

The Power of 1440

MAKING THE MOST OF EVERY MINUTE IN A DAY

Tim Timberlake

with Keith Wall

W PUBLISHING GROUP

AN IMPRINT OF THOMAS NELSON

The Power of 1440

© 2021 Tim Timberlake

All rights reserved. No portion of this book may be reproduced, stored in a retrieval system, or transmitted in any form or by any means—electronic, mechanical, photocopy, recording, scanning, or other—except for brief quotations in critical reviews or articles, without the prior written permission of the publisher.

Published in Nashville, Tennessee, by W Publishing, an imprint of Thomas Nelson.

Published in association with The Bindery Agency, www.TheBinderyAgency.com.

Thomas Nelson titles may be purchased in bulk for educational, business, fundraising, or sales promotional use. For information, please email SpecialMarkets@ThomasNelson.com.

Unless otherwise noted, Scripture quotations taken from The Holy Bible, New International Version®, NIV®. Copyright © 1973, 1978, 1984, 2011 by Biblica, Inc.® Used by permission of Zondervan. All rights reserved worldwide. www. Zondervan.com. The "NIV" and "New International Version" are trademarks registered in the United States Patent and Trademark Office by Biblica, Inc.®

Scripture quotations marked ESV are taken from the ESV® Bible (The Holy Bible, English Standard Version®). Copyright © 2001 by Crossway, a publishing ministry of Good News Publishers. Used by permission. All rights reserved.

Scripture quotations marked MSG are taken from *THE MESSAGE*. Copyright © 1993, 2002, 2018 by Eugene H. Peterson. Used by permission of NavPress. All rights reserved. Represented by Tyndale House Publishers, Inc.

Scripture quotations marked NASB are taken from the New American Standard Bible® (NASB). Copyright © 1960, 1962, 1963, 1968, 1971, 1972, 1973, 1975, 1977, 1995 by The Lockman Foundation. Used by permission. www.lockman.org

Scripture quotations marked NKJV are taken from the New King James Version®. Copyright © 1982 by Thomas Nelson. Used by permission. All rights reserved.

Scripture quotations marked NLT are taken from the Holy Bible, New Living Translation. © 1996, 2004, 2015 by Tyndale House Foundation. Used by permission of Tyndale House Publishers, Inc., Carol Stream, Illinois 60188. All rights reserved.

Scripture quotations marked TLB are taken from The Living Bible. Copyright © 1971. Used by permission of Tyndale House Publishers, Inc., Carol Stream, Illinois 60188. All rights reserved.

Any internet addresses, phone numbers, or company or product information printed in this book are offered as a resource and are not intended in any way to be or to imply an endorsement by Thomas Nelson, nor does Thomas Nelson vouch for the existence, content, or services of these sites, phone numbers, companies, or products beyond the life of this book.

ISBN 978-0-7852-3894-2 (audiobook)
ISBN 978-0-7852-3893-5 (eBook)

Library of Congress Control Number: 2020943244

ISBN 978-0-7852-3892-8

Printed in the United States of America

21 22 23 24 25 LSC 10 9 8 7 6 5 4 3 2 1

To Jennifer, the love of my life

A NOTE TO THE READER

My prayer as you read through the pages of this book is that you will experience incredible moments, the kind you will look back on and pinpoint as the catalyst that led you one step closer to the beauty and adventure that comes with living out the power and potential of each day.

CONTENTS

Foreword by John Maxwell   xv
Savor: The Art of Relishing the Moment   xvii

1. The Power of One Day   1
2. Everyday Extraordinary   7
3. Seven Days of Splendor   13
4. Vu Déjà   20
5. "I'll Be the One"   25
6. Mess into Miracles   32
7. Know Where You Want to Go   38
8. Out of Control   43
9. Nothing Changes If Nothing Changes   49
10. Cultivate Contentment During Scarcity   57
11. Keep Perspective Through Plenty   64
12. To Move Beyond, Leave It Behind   69
13. Master the Moment   76
14. Rest to Give Your Best   83
15. Face Your Fear   89
16. Today, Give Yourself Away   101
17. Destiny in a Day   107
18. Transformed Through Transparency   113
19. Defeat Your Doubts   119
20. The Power of Perspective   126

21. Follow the Leader 132
22. Find Freedom in Forgiveness 138
23. Motive Matters 143
24. Step One 149
25. Bad Day, Good Heart 154
26. Master of One 159
27. Miraculous Disaster 164
28. Food Inspector 169
29. Wait Training 178
30. The Magnificent Map 183

No Time to Waste 189
Acknowledgments 191
Notes 195
About the Author 202

FOREWORD

What if I told you that you already have everything you need to make a godly impact in the world? You've already been given every single tool that you need. And you've been given 1440 of them to be exact.

This leadership book will rock your perspective, it will radically shift how you approach each day, and ultimately, it could change your life.

In early 2020, I had the honor and privilege to spend some time with Tim Timberlake at a leadership roundtable. We had the opportunity to talk about our lives, and how they connected even though I hadn't known it. Tim shared that his father, the late Bishop Mack Timberlake, had given my book *Developing the Leader Within You* to Tim as a gift in the summer of 1994. We spoke at length about our Savior, Jesus, and Tim also shared about this book, which had been stirring in his heart for a long time. This book has finally come to fruition, and at the perfect time. As Tim shared with me the principles of *The Power of 1440*, I knew it was special.

The Power of 1440 is a refreshing approach to making the most out of the 1440 minutes that are gifted to each of us every day. This book is practical and relatable, and simple at its core—as only you and I are responsible for making the most of what God has given to us.

Tim unpacks how many of us have been conditioned to wake up begrudgingly and go about our days without truly understanding the richness God intended for our lives. Rather than living in the present sometimes we get stuck in a cyclical pattern of depression, anger, fear, worry, regret, or boredom—but we don't have to stay there!

Tim Timberlake is the voice we need in this season. A voice of encouragement, change, and possibility. No matter what stage of life you find yourself in, this message will stir something within you.

I encourage you to grab a fresh notebook and a highlighter as you dive in to read. This book is great to use as a daily refresh in your routine. Start each day with a plan for how you will use the 1440 minutes entrusted to you!

—John C. Maxwell

SAVOR: THE ART OF RELISHING THE MOMENT

You and I are granted 1440 minutes each day, a gift from God offered for us to use fully and fruitfully, to savor, and to seize. For all of us, every day contains these 1440 opportunities to experience abundance and fulfillment as well as generosity and self-sacrifice.

I am passionate about sharing this message with you because I have learned the extraordinary value and gift of each minute that comes with every day. But as with many essential life lessons, I learned this one the hard way. A moment can come and go without our recognizing its power, potential, or eternal significance. It happened to me one particular time in a way that makes me never want to forget the lessons of our moments. I remember it like it was yesterday.

When I was twelve years old, my father and I went to a shopping center in the fashion district in Los Angeles and sat down for a quick lunch. Dad and I both loved hot dogs. I mean absolutely loved to the point of considering ourselves connoisseurs. So that's what we decided to eat. As we settled in for our first bites, an odd thing happened: my father couldn't open his mouth enough to eat. My first thought was lockjaw. Though we didn't think that was possible, we both became concerned, wondering what was going on. He asked me to massage his neck, and after I did, he was able to chew.

From that point on his problem grew worse. It was clear that *something* was affecting his throat. He finally made an appointment with his physician, who told him and my mom that their hectic traveling schedule was causing the problem. My parents, Mack and Brenda Timberlake, were both pastors who preached several times a week in various cities. They were renowned worldwide, preaching the gospel continually in person and on television. Even so, my dad listened to the doctor and curtailed his traveling schedule, but the pain and throat issues did not improve. In fact, they grew worse.

My father, still without clear answers, went to an ear, nose, and throat specialist. The moment the doctor put a scope down his throat was a moment that would forever change our lives.

The ENT told my father he had a tumor in his throat the size of a chipmunk. He *immediately* needed to check himself into a hospital for surgery. After some testing, it was later determined to be terminal stage-four cancer. Some days went by before he underwent an eight-hour surgery, followed by countless rounds of chemo and radiation, all in an attempt to remove the large cancerous tumor. The process ravaged his body, leaving him clinging to life, with only a portion of his tongue.

This didn't make sense. I had never seen my dad do any wrong. He was the epitome of a Christlike man, preaching the Word of God far and wide. And most important, behind closed doors, around the people who mattered most to him, he lived out what he preached. So this sudden health crisis was confusing. How could God allow this?

I watched my father go from a strapping six foot, four inches and 280 pounds to a straggly 170 pounds. And because part of his tongue was removed during the surgery, he couldn't eat or drink through his mouth. He was fed a liquid diet through a gastrostomy tube placed in his stomach. Despite his discomfort, and though it looked on the outside like his life was wasting away, he still steadfastly preached the Word of God. But as his health continued to worsen, he became so weak I eventually had to dress him. On Sundays, after I put his clothes on him, he would go to church and preach, always determined to help as many people as possible by teaching about God's grace and love.

Despite the example of my father's deep faith, my doubts about God grew. *How could a loving heavenly Father allow my beloved earthly father to suffer so much? How could this warrior of the faith, a paragon of virtue and integrity, be abandoned in his hour of greatest need by the God he served?*

I became distant from the God my father so adamantly talked about, a prodigal son of sorts, living for myself and running in the opposite direction of the foundational truths my parents had taught me. I couldn't help but wonder, *If my godly father could be hit with such a terrible disease, what did God have in store for me, with all my many flaws?*

Fast-forward five years. My father had been in and out of the hospital, enduring surgeries, chemotherapy, and radiation. I was seventeen and visiting West Palm Beach, Florida, doing a number of things I probably had no business doing. While there, I received an urgent call from my mother that my father had been hospitalized and had passed away. I frantically rushed home to figure out what had happened and to be with my mother.

To my utter shock, I came back to find my dad was still alive. He'd had a near-death event and flatlined, but he had been resuscitated. Afterward he told my mom that he could not go home to heaven until he had a chance to talk with me about what it means to be a man, especially a man of God.

A few days later my father sat me down for that talk. He told me what it takes to be a real man. He talked to me about his faith in God and what it means to follow Jesus. He shared with me his thoughts about marriage, family, parenting, ministry, and friendship. Thinking back to it now, it reminds me of the sacred Old Testament practice of a father sitting down with his son (in the story it was his firstborn son), offering his blessing, and passing down the birthright.

We talked for *five* hours. In those sacred moments, Dad poured out his heart and told me everything I needed to know about life, love, faith, and calling. He talked openly about his dreams, disappointments, successes, and setbacks. As rich as that time together was, to be honest, I wasn't paying very close attention to everything he said. Since he had miraculously recovered and was speaking to me as lucidly as ever, I thought we'd have many more conversations together. I thought I had more time with him. I was wrong.

When our discussion ended, my father went to bed. That same night my mother woke me at 2:00 a.m. to tell me my father was incoherent and unresponsive. We called the EMTs, but before they arrived, my father passed from this world to heaven.

I knew then I had to step up and be the man I was raised to be. I may have had my doubts, but my father never did. And through his faith, my faith grew. The faith of my father laid the groundwork for my faith.

I'll be real and genuine with you about that final conversation with my father. I feel deep regret because of that missed opportunity. If I could relive those five final hours with my dad, I would be 100 percent fully focused, like a student listening to a beloved master teacher. I would have a notebook in my lap, writing down every pearl of wisdom and every morsel of sage advice. I would be a sponge, soaking in every word, lesson, and encouragement. But I didn't. And now I realize those hours—those three hundred minutes—were a turning point in my life that I largely let pass by. That day was also my eighteenth birthday, a day that will forever be burned into my memory and a day I'll always wish I could get back.

The good news is that experience taught me an essential principle of life and faith: I will try, to the best of my ability, to never again let an opportunity slip by unnoticed and unheeded. I certainly have moments, like everyone, when I am distracted and preoccupied, but I make every effort to seize each minute and heed the guidance of Scripture:

- "Be very careful, then, how you live—not as unwise but as wise, making the most of every opportunity." (Eph. 5:15–16)
- "Make the most of every opportunity." (Col. 4:5)
- "Teach us to number our days, that we may gain a heart of wisdom." (Ps. 90:12)
- "But make sure that you don't get so absorbed and exhausted in taking care of all your day-by-day obligations that you lose track of the time and doze off, oblivious to God. . . . We can't afford to waste a minute." (Rom. 13:11, 13 MSG)

These scriptures embody the spirit in which I share the message of 1440: making the most of every God-given minute of every single day. As we walk together through the following thirty chapters, or if you'd like to read a chapter a day over the next thirty days, let's lean in and learn how to fully savor and maximize the potential packed into each minute of every single day we are given.

You'll read about some of the tools I've collected on my journey, things that have never failed me as I've faced the endless surprises of life. You may notice that some of the principles come back again and again. Each time a new facet is revealed, and each time we discover unexpected power in them. Things like gratitude, excellence, generosity, and mindfulness. These are like keys on your key chain that open lock after lock, freeing you to open the potential of each one of the 1440 minutes in your day. So I encourage you to explore them all and dive into the ones that resonate with you most. From beginning to end, I hope the minutes we spend together inspire you to make the very most of yours.

ONE

THE POWER OF ONE DAY

There is priceless treasure ready for the taking right before your eyes.

Let me tell you about a number. One thousand four hundred forty, to be precise.

1440

These four simple yet infinitely ample digits changed my life. That's a big claim, I know, but it's true. This number opened my eyes to possibilities and reminded me that God wants me to enjoy a magnificent life, not a mediocre one.

Trust me, I'm nobody special, so I can promise without hesitation this number will change your life too. I've got nothing to sell but hope, nothing to gain but the better world we will build together. If you take a moment to slow your mind and bring yourself to a place of complete focus, I would like to tell you about this number.

- 1440 is not an exclusive Park Avenue address for the wealthy and powerful, *but I guarantee it will enrich your life in ways you can barely begin to imagine.*

- 1440 is not some pivotal date in the history of humankind, *but if you embrace its meaning, your world will never be the same.*
- 1440 is not how many daily calories you are allowed on the latest fad diet, *but it can lift a heavy weight off your shoulders and renew your strength.*
- 1440 is not the amount of money it will cost you to learn the secrets of success from some fast-talking expert *because this door is open to anyone who knocks.*

While it's not any of those things, 1440 is the exact number of daily golden opportunities God gives to each and every one of us as freely as the air we breathe and the sunshine that warms us. Not just once, at birth, in a limited supply with strict instructions to make it last. Not just on special occasions when we might beg extra hard for a divine blessing or commit an act of extraordinary charity to earn a heavenly bonus.

Nothing like that.

Your Creator gives you 1440 invitations to grab hold of a life that is more abundant and more joyful than anything you've ever experienced. Every. Single. Day.

Dawn to dawn, inclusive of those essential times of resting and recharging, 1440 is the number of chances every single person on earth has to make *this* day truly extraordinary.

If you are breathing, then there is no way to get caught at the back of the line at closing time and miss out on your portion of 1440 minutes. While you live, no one else can steal them from you. It doesn't matter who you are, what you've done, the color of your skin, the language you speak, or the religion of your culture. Everyone receives the same deposit of time each day. There is only one person on earth who can take the 1440 heavenly jewels meant to make you rich and bury them in the sand.

You.

So many of us do exactly that.

Show of hands. Who has ever opened your eyes on a new day and inwardly (or outwardly) groaned in dread? Who has ever found it difficult to get out of bed under a crushing weight of fear, worry, doubt, distraction, depression, regret, hopelessness, or just plain boredom? Right. *Everyone.*

There are reasons for that, reasons we are conditioned to look at our 1440 minutes as a burden rather than the priceless treasure they truly are. Some of those reasons are the artifacts of modern life. It isn't easy to navigate the fast-paced demands of our technological society. But that isn't the whole story. This book is devoted to revealing the other causes for our distress—the ones we impose upon ourselves—and then to shouting out loud how we can stop! And how we can step up and step out into greatness one minute at a time.

TILLING THE FERTILE SOIL OF YOUR LIFE

In the following chapters we will explore the many hands-on ways to put potential into practice and make every day live up to God's original intent. His original plan was each day would be better than good. The type of day that leaves you satisfied, knowing that you've squeezed every moment of greatness out of it.

But before setting out, let's pack up a few ideas you'll need to succeed at everything that follows.

TODAY IS ALL YOU'VE GOT

Those words—Today is all you've got—are more than the caption on a cat poster or a slogan on a meme. They are more than an inspirational thought on a greeting card.

Trying to unlock the power of 1440 in your life without understanding the truth of "today is all you've got" would be like trying to start your car without the key. It's theoretically possible but a whole lot harder. Here's what you need to know.

The past is gone. Totally beyond your reach or your ability to control. You can try to repair damage done in the past or relive a moment that was pleasurable—*but only today.*

The future is a *fantasy* and also completely outside your grasp. You can prepare for the tomorrow you want or take steps to avoid one you'd rather not live through *today and nowhere else.*

Sure, your personality is made up of your memories and your aspirations. But the part of your life you actually *live*, without exception, is the part happening right in front of you right now.

Imagine you are going on a trip tomorrow. You can pack your bag today, plan what you will do when you get there, buy a ticket, and book an Uber to the airport. But there is *no way* to get on the plane and travel across country until tomorrow. That moment has to arrive in the present before you can live it, so why bother trying? That's what worry is about: trying to live a moment that is either long gone or hasn't yet arrived.

Why is it so important to grasp this fact? Because your biggest enemies in the quest for a more abundant and rewarding life can seem like big, bad warlords who are seriously entrenched in these two provinces of your mind: the past and the future. Time—any time but the present—is the part of your life occupied by all your worry, fear, doubt, anxiety, guilt, anger, boredom, and regret. Try to live *there* instead of today, and more often than not you'll take a beating from thoughts that don't serve you now.

Today is the day you are meant to live. Now is the inheritance that is yours to spend.

YOU ARE IN CHARGE

No one can choose for you how you spend your 1440 gold coins. No one else can decide what thoughts you give your attention to or which actions you invest your energy in. It's up to you.

If your life is stagnant and disappointing, then everything you need to turn things around is right at your fingertips in the 1440 minutes in this day. But *you* have to decide to put them to use. Think of it this way: a computer is the most powerful tool ever created, but until you turn it on, put your hands to work on the keys, and engage your mind with a clear vision of what you want to do, it's little more than an expensive paperweight.

Every one of your 1440 minutes today contains the potential to transform your life and the world around you if *you* choose to make it so.

THE CURRENCY OF CHANGE IS BELIEF

No one in the history of the world ever accomplished anything they didn't believe was possible. Otherwise, how would they face and overcome the challenges and inevitable setbacks along the way? How could they justify an investment of time, energy, and resources into a project they believed was doomed to failure?

The truth is, the world reflects back to us our own vision of reality. Do you expect mostly failures and hardships in your life? If so, that's what you'll get. Some people see this as evidence that God is indifferent to your suffering. But I'd invite you to reread the previous point: *you* are in charge of your own experience of life. It's not indifference God shows to us but the gift of freedom and confidence in our ability to live up to our potential as children made in his image.

Belief is the currency and the current, the power source that plugs you into the whole awesome, revolutionary potential contained in 1440. If the world you want doesn't match the world you see in your deepest thoughts, then resolve to renew your belief in what God said of the universe when creation was complete: *It is good!*

QUIT SETTLING FOR LESS

No matter who you are, the garden of your life can become choked with the weeds of sloppy habits, mistaken beliefs, untrue thoughts, and a weird kind of mental stubbornness that refuses to believe life can be any other way. Mine was and, if I'm honest about it, still is from time to time.

But I've seen the power of 1440 for myself, and I don't want to settle for anything less than extraordinary any longer in my life and in my world. God never meant for our lives to be mean or hard or full of struggle and lack. We are intended to be unbelievably fruitful, joyful, healthy, happy, and whole. Believe it! It's as if you have been given 1440 seeds in the minutes of your day. Enough to grow an extraordinary, flourishing garden in your life.

I know you are ready to stop settling too. So let's gather our tools, put on our gloves, get down on our knees, and start digging. I'm excited to see what we'll grow together *today*!

TWO

EVERYDAY EXTRAORDINARY

Shift your mindset from mundane to miraculous.

I have a crazy confession to make. I have lived most of my life under the spell of a terrible bias. These days that's not an easy thing to admit. I'd like to believe I'm smart enough and mature enough to be free of all kinds of biased and blinkered thinking. In most respects I suppose that's true, but in this case I've been as backward and limited in my thinking as anyone.

As with most predisposed perspectives, the telltale evidence lies in the language I use. Words always have a way of revealing and betraying my true attitudes and beliefs. That's because words are always reflections of one's core beliefs.

Here's one particular word that is evidence of my bias: *ordinary*. I'm guilty of thoughtlessly using this adjective to mislabel and malign most of the golden moments I'm given each day. It is an ungrateful, dismissive word that drags along with it a string of others: trivial, mediocre, insignificant, boring, normal.

"Ordinary life" is the biased way I have often characterized everything that happens in my life between getting out of bed in the morning and back into it at night. I've fantasized about being, doing, or having something *extra*ordinary, something above and beyond what already is, if only I could escape the tyranny of the mundane.

The best defense I can offer is that I'm far from alone with this bias. Humans all seem prone to using the word *ordinary* as it's defined in the *Oxford English Dictionary*, namely, to mean "with no special or distinctive features."[1] Read that out loud. What a sobering reminder that this thought pattern is a sad, sorry way in which to view ourselves and our lives! It's hardly surprising, however, since we are immersed, practically from day one, in a torrent of cultural messaging that reinforces this tragic way of thinking. Marketers and manipulators of all kinds do a brisk trade in dissatisfaction in order to fill a manufactured need with merchandise and empty experiences.

If all of this sounds familiar to you, and if you've grown as tired as I am of living in a constant state of restless discontent, then today could be a game changer for you. I have great news! We each have the power, and perhaps even the duty, to uproot this old way of seeing the world. We can plant a radical and liberating truth in its place. Here it is: *There is no such thing as ordinary. Not a single second of your life or mine could ever be anything other than fantastically full of power, beauty, meaning, purpose, and potential.*

Not. A. Single. Second.

Why? The truth is, ordinary doesn't exist, because every moment of your life is a gift from God himself. It is not a matter of wondering whether God *would* give his children anything less than the best of everything (he would not!), but whether such a thing is even possible. *It is not!* As Jesus told his followers, "Which of you fathers, if your son asks for a fish, will give him a snake instead? Or if he asks for an egg, will give him a scorpion? If you then, though you are evil, know how to give good gifts to your children, how much more will your Father in heaven give the Holy Spirit to those who ask him!" (Luke 11:11–13).

The writers of the Old Testament understood a powerful truth that we should remember ourselves: "The LORD our God, the LORD is one"

(Deut. 6:4). That means there is nothing *but* God, and he is nothing but good. He inhabits his creation. He is involved in every human situation. He loves his children. He lives within his people—including you!

When you really think about it, every moment he gives us is extraordinary. Good moments become good memories. And bad moments, if viewed from the right perspective, become good lessons.

WHAT MATTERS IS YOUR MIND

But hang on a minute. If God truly lives within us, if his miraculous and mind-blowing handiwork is visible in every created thing, if the world truly hums with the energy of the human potential for greatness, then why do so many of us hang our heads in melancholy and malaise as if existence is some kind of permanent after-school detention? We act like we're all assigned to a life that's to be lived in a dull and dreary room and made to write the same sentence over and over. A clock ticks sluggishly on the wall while we all stare out a window and yearn for release and freedom.

Why do we put ourselves in detention? To find the answer, look no further than your own mind. That's the only place God's creation can appear to be anything other than magnificent, because it is where we insist on imagining things to be other than they truly are. The only reason life ever seems ordinary, or even burdensome, is because we choose to think it is. We *believe* it to be true and so it is.

This is the obvious flip side of what Jesus taught: "Truly, I say to you, whoever says to this mountain, 'Be taken up and thrown into the sea,' and does not doubt in his heart, but believes that what he says will come to pass, it will be done for him" (Mark 11:23 ESV). I'd much rather be doing that kind of thing than sitting in detention, wouldn't you?

If firm belief in the miraculous can bestow such power, then inverted thoughts of limitation, lack, and fear can create the opposite effect in your life. Our lives will always move in the direction of our strongest and most dominant thoughts. Every miracle or breakthrough begins in the seeds sown in the ground of your imagination.

The choice is yours. You can train your mind to see the marvelous presence of God in everything or focus on the dreary. Don't get caught in the trap of sorting life into artificial categories called "ordinary" and "special."

The path you take—and keep on taking until it becomes second nature—determines your *mindset*, the sum of your beliefs and assumptions about yourself and the world. What and how you think is up to you.

Hear me when I tell you this is incredibly good news! It means you already possess the key to unlock the door between you and your freedom from a mediocre life. With a shift in your mindset— from *mundane* to *miraculous*—you can throw open the doors of the detention hall, dance down the hallway, and burst out onto a bustling playground of extraordinary living.

BREAKING THE ORDINARY HABIT

It's time to lose that ingrained habit of assuming your life is ordinary. You might think one brick is ordinary, but put enough of them together and you've got a soaring cathedral. And you can build yours one brick at a time by just showing up every day determined to lay that brick in a pattern that makes something extraordinary.

As easy as that is to do, we both know what is easy to do is also easy *not* to do. Your thoughts are entrenched and are used to having the last word. It takes determination and effort to regain the upper hand. But it is possible!

Whenever my thought pattern starts to slip back into the discouragingly mundane, I turn to the words of the apostle Paul: "Do not be conformed to this world, but be transformed by the renewal of your mind, that by testing you may discern what is the will of God, what is good and acceptable and perfect" (Rom. 12:2 ESV). If we do not correct our minds before we go into a new day, a new opportunity, or a new season, we'll keep reliving the same story. We will take bricks from our past and build the same house in our future.

Which brings us to the question, "How do we get a renewed mind?" Let's begin by comparing and contrasting how these opposing mindsets cause you to think.

THE MUNDANE MINDSET

- **Thinks God is far away.** If it's your habit to picture a detached God who is watching the world from some distant place, then it's easier to believe a life of significance is out of reach as well.
- **Focuses only on what is lacking.** This way of thinking assumes there is never enough to go around. The mundane mindset prods you to expect shortage and every other kind of trouble too.
- **Sees time as an obstacle.** In an ordinary worldview, there is always either too little time or too much. Believing time is in short supply is stressful, while an overabundance of it leads to a sense of drudgery and boredom.
- **Focuses on what can't be done.** If you think it's impossible, you make it impossible. The mundane mentality preempts greatness by endlessly worrying over all the things that will never work.
- **Feels entitled to more than what is.** Ordinary-minded people use the words *should* and *shouldn't* a lot to describe all the things they believe keep them trapped in a less-than-extraordinary life.
- **Confuses spectacle with special.** Mass media has made the spectacular seem normal. Unlike what we are accustomed to seeing on TV, the present moment is rarely accompanied by fireworks and orchestral music, so it's easy to conclude it has no special or distinctive features.

11

- **Feels bound by limitations.** Even when the mundane mindset dares to dream, its perceived reality can seem like a malicious jailer determined to thwart your every chance.

THE MIRACULOUS MINDSET

- **Sees God's presence in everything.** Morning sunlight through a window. The smell of coffee in the kitchen. The companionship of someone you love. Birdsong outside. Each moment is positively littered with evidence of God's nearness to those who are awake and aware.
- **Counts every blessing.** Far from seeing the cup of their life as half empty, this person knows it overflows with good things.
- **Treats each moment as perfect.** To the miracle minded, there is no need to ever race against time or to kill time. Now is always sufficient.
- **Believes anything is possible.** Of course it is!
- **Is grateful for everything.** Nothing opens the door to faith in possibility like giving thanks for what has already been given to you.
- **Sees the value in seemingly small things.** In fact, the renewed mind no longer believes in such limiting words. Every gift is good regardless of its size or appearance.
- **Expects every door to open.** "Ask, and it will be given to you; seek, and you will find; knock, and it will be opened to you" (Matt. 7:7 ESV). When we seek to live out the will of God while also seeking to align our heart with his, he will indeed answer our prayers in a way that is the very best for our lives.

Begin today noticing where your mind is. If your habit has been to dwell on limitation and lack and to expect nothing but an ordinary life, don't despair! You have the power to move the meter from the mundane to the miraculous whenever you choose to do so.

THREE

SEVEN DAYS
OF SPLENDOR

Each day of the week (even Monday!)
is overflowing with possibilities.

If there's a song that serves as the soundtrack for people through-
out our society, it might be the 1981 classic by the band Loverboy,
"Working for the Weekend." Or for those who prefer a little funk
in their playlist, it might be the O'Jays' 1976 hit "Livin' for the
Weekend." Or others might choose the more recent Coldplay song
"Hymn for the Weekend."

I could go on and on citing songs about the joys of weekends
as well as disdain for workdays. There are just as many songs about
hating Mondays as there are about loving weekends.

This shouldn't surprise us because Mondays have, over the decades, developed a reputation for drudgery and misery. And the days
immediately following don't fare much better. It's as if we've become
conditioned to accept Monday through Thursday as days to endure
and tolerate while we wait for Friday through Sunday to enjoy and
celebrate.

Journalist Julia Guerra sums up the attitude of many people:
"We all loathe Mondays and love Fridays. Weekends symbolize

freedom and plans with loved ones, while Tuesday through Thursday are usually all about work. It's easy to forget what day it is when there's nothing particularly interesting going on."[1]

So what does a typical week look like for you? What characterizes each day? Here's a rundown of some common perceptions:

Monday: Universally reviled and resisted, this much-maligned day is the bane of people throughout the land: employed and self-employed, interns and CEOs, students and teachers. It's no wonder we frequently hear people talk about having the Monday blues or a case of the Mondays.

Tuesday: This day might be considered "Monday with a hangover." Not quite as bad as Monday, but still a long way from the weekend.

Wednesday: Hump day! Normally a typical day, ho-hum and uneventful, the end of the day on Wednesday is a bright spot for many, meaning they've gotten past the week's halfway point.

Thursday: Sometimes referred to as Friday Eve, Thursday is another grind-it-out day, but one that has inched closer to the weekend, offering hope to those ready for the workweek to end and playtime to begin.

Friday: TGIF! Even though it is technically a workday, this day is usually heralded as the start of the weekend.

Saturday: Sleep in, leisurely sip your coffee, make pancakes for the kids. It's a day to slow your pace, catch up on chores, and spend the day in sweats. Whatever you choose, it's usually a day of downtime and playtime.

Sunday: God designed one day of the week to be a sabbath, set aside for rest and worship. People of faith usually attend church services and participate with their faith community. This day, for many people, is also devoted to football, golf, and backyard barbecues.

TODAY IS THE DAY

We miss many opportunities to thrive, grow, and shine when we prioritize one day over another and categorize days as either good or bad. If you begin a day, any day, believing it's going to be lousy, it likely will be! Your attitude will determine your productivity, performance, and peace of mind.

If we muddle through Monday, presuming it's the worst day of the week, we won't view it as a fresh start. If we trudge through Tuesday, already looking toward the weekend, our outlook and disposition will be compromised. If we whine about Wednesday, waiting to get over the hump, we will miss opportunities to bless others and be blessed ourselves. If we are tepid about Thursday, anticipating Friday as a fun day, we won't be present and focused on today's possibilities.

To maximize each of our 1440 daily minutes, we need to view every day as an invitation to create, produce, and flourish. To make the most of each day, we should wake up in the morning and anticipate God's leading to encourage and empower others. To seize the power of today, we ought to believe we will grow and develop on that day.

Every minute we have the opportunity, if we will see it and seize it, to step closer to our God-given potential and live out our faith with hearts full of enthusiasm. Our attitude should be guided by a psalm: "This is the day that the LORD has made; let us rejoice and be glad in it" (118:24 ESV).

MAKE MONDAY THROUGH SUNDAY MAGNIFICENT

Plenty of things consume our time and distract us from making the most of each day. We are the ones who decide whether or not to live fully Monday through Sunday. Someone wisely said, "Life is not measured by the number of breaths we take, but by the moments that take our breath away."[2] What takes your breath away? If you aren't sure how to live each day with passion and purpose, start with these strategies.

LAUGH OFTEN

Most people mistakenly believe laughter is like water from a faucet; that is, only a happy feeling can turn it on. Cause and effect. Feeling comes first, then comes the smiling and laughing.

The truth is, researchers have discovered that laughter and genuine joyfulness are two sides of an equation that works in both directions.[3] Sure, spontaneous laughter is fun. But in less happy moments there is power in choosing to smile or laugh, because emotion has a way of following with measurable mental and physical health benefits. So-called laughter yoga (the practice of laughing on purpose) has become increasingly popular in recent years. Invariably, what begins as forced joyfulness turns into the real thing and is highly contagious.[4]

CHOOSE TO BE GENEROUS

Like the bumper sticker says, "Practice Random Acts of Kindness."[5] But the key word is not *random*. It is *practice*. That's because, like laughter, generosity is not always our first impulse. We all have our own problems, which can feel overwhelming and push thoughts of "doing unto others" right out of our minds. It takes practice and determination to make generosity a part of who you are.

There is good reason to do so. As author Og Mandino wrote, "Remember that there is no happiness in having or in getting, but only in giving. Reach out. Share. Smile. Hug. Happiness is a perfume you cannot pour on others without getting a few drops on yourself."[6] It's true that making someone else happy is a very good way to lift your own spirits too.

GUARD YOUR THOUGHTS AND WORDS

An ancient proverb says, "As above, so below. As within, so without."[7] When it comes to creating more joy in your life, this wisdom can help guide the way, because it reminds us that the world we experience on the outside is directly linked to the quality of our inner world, where our internal dialogue shapes the landscape.

If you indulge a constant stream of negative and critical thoughts, you are unlikely to feel much joy in living or to inspire it in others. That's even truer if you make a habit of putting those thoughts into spoken words.

Pay attention to your mental chatter, and steer it toward gratitude and positive affirmations about yourself and others. You'll be shocked how much lighter and more joyful your life becomes.

So ease up on negative self-talk. We all have an inner voice that constantly blabbers about our faults and failings as well as pessimistic messages about the day ahead. But you control the on-off switch for that voice. It has had its way for so long that it may take work to regain access to the controls. But you can. Replace negative abstractions with positive affirmations. Instead of saying, "Today is going to be a nightmare," say, "I've got what it takes to meet the challenges." Instead of "I'm never going to get through this work by the end of the day," tell yourself, "I have enough time and enough energy to finish what I need to do."

CULTIVATE GRATITUDE FOR EACH NEW DAY

In an intriguing article titled "Mondays Don't Suck, Your Perception Does," author Yvette Brown observed, "Mondays signify a new week. Don't take that for granted. To say you have made it to another Monday is no small feat. Whether it's because you got insanely irresponsible during your weekend or simply because right now the world we live in is so crazy, being blessed with another day to live, get things right, and be productive should be at the top of your gratitude list. Last week might have sucked. It might have been unproductive. But guess what? You were granted a clean slate so maybe that's a sign that you can get things right!"[8]

This is true not just for Mondays but every day. You have been given a new start, a fresh beginning by God each morning. Don't overlook this gift. Receive it with gratitude and utilize it fully.

MOVE BEYOND MEDIOCRITY

The word *mediocrity* derives from the Latin *medius*, meaning middle or medium. Mediocrity is the quality or state of being ordinary, average, commonplace, run of the mill. It is that midway point between high and low, success and failure, greatness and incompetence, ferocity and docility. However else you might define the word, *mediocre* is not a label we would want applied to *us*. Yet we often make little effort to rise above and pursue greatness.

Mediocrity is essentially a quality of being halfhearted, dispassionate, and perfunctory. It often results from applying only a moderate amount of what we are capable of on any given dimension.

So when we ask ourselves if we're settling for mediocrity in any way, we're really asking, Am I maximizing my potential? Am I thoroughly utilizing my energy and abilities? Or am I too laidback and lackadaisical? Could I do more and be more if I mobilized my resources more fully?

HERE ARE THREE THINGS YOU CAN DO TO MAXIMIZE POTENTIAL

1. **Set a mental target.** Productivity experts suggest retroactively putting things on a to-do list just so you can check things off. But I had to stop doing that. Every method doesn't work for everybody, and that method didn't work for me. These days I rank in numerical order the top things that must be done

ASAP, generally big projects. From there, I assign a time when they need to be done. Hard deadlines for me are the biggest motivators to get those items done.

2. **Remain positive.** How we think determines our perspective, and our perspective determines our experiences. Being intentional about staying positive will help you maximize and overhaul your thinking.

3. **Transcend what you cannot control.** The reality of our lives is this: we can control very little of it. We may think we are in control, but we are not. Once we come to the realization that we cannot control what happens from day to day, then we find the necessary power in trusting the One who controls everything.

The Bible gives us hope and the knowledge that we, as God's children, can wake up each day to blessings large and small. When we take notice of that and grab hold of the powerful truth that God stands in our yesterday, today, and tomorrow, we will see that, with the help of God, life can be full of all the splendor we hadn't known before. There is something for you to treasure today and every day.

FOUR

VU DÉJÀ

*Everyday experiences become
fresh and remarkable when
viewed with childlike wonder.*

Have you ever found yourself in the middle of an activity and had the odd feeling that you've lived that exact moment before? At the same time, you know it's impossible. Perhaps you're talking with someone you've never met before or visiting a place for the first time. And yet the feeling is undeniable.

In a moment of déjà vu, a new experience feels old. *This seems so familiar*, you think, *but I'm sure this never happened before.* Sixty to seventy percent of us have experienced déjà vu, and perhaps you are one of them.[1]

I've reversed the words and named this chapter "Vu Déjà" because I want you to experience the opposite of déjà vu. I don't want *new* experiences to feel *old*. Instead, I long for you to feel that something you do all the time—a regular, recurring experience you might be tempted to think of as mundane—is new and exciting. I want even your routine days to feel infused with a sense of uniqueness and excitement and untapped potential.

WOULDN'T IT BE AMAZING TO LIVE THIS WAY?

We're all charmed by the way kids approach life, aren't we? Toddlers and young kids have a way of finding delight in even the most routine events. My three-year-old son Max can grab a stick in our backyard and instantly become a sword-wielding knight fending off villains. He can spot a bug on our living room carpet and envision it's on an epic journey to a magical land.

My point is that kids find delight in a lot of stuff that you and I—serious adults that we are—consider real yawners. I realize that most grown-ups might feel hesitant to play knights in the yard and wouldn't devote much time to staring at a bug. But I believe we would all be better off if we recaptured some of the feelings of delight, adventure, and possibility that children feel every single day.

It's no wonder that Jesus emphasized the theme of living with childlike wonder several times, as when he told his serious-minded disciples, "Unless you change and become like little children, you will never enter the kingdom of heaven" (Matt. 18:3). Paradise belongs to children and the childlike, the young and the young at heart.

To kick-start that kind of energizing shift, we need simply to view our routine, ordinary experiences with the fresh, new view that a child might have. The following three shifts might seem subtle at first but can be game changers as you seek to make the most of every minute of your day.

PRACTICE PEERING THROUGH THE EYES OF OTHERS

Every so often I engage in an exercise to remind myself that choosing to view things differently is valuable. Suppose I'm sitting at my desk, looking at my water bottle. I close one eye and then open it. Next, I close the other eye. I repeat this, watching for subtle differences in what I see. The bottle of water might be closer to my computer when observed through my left eye than my right.

Then I touch my nose with my finger and repeat the eye thing. The views of my hand from my left and right eyes are even more interesting than the shifting bottle of water. It's pretty fascinating, the difference, when all I've done is shift my point of view three inches to the right or left.

Try it for yourself. What if you could see things from a position much greater in distance? Or even completely different in nature? What if you could see through the eyes of a different history, experience, or attitude than your own? Through the eyes of an entirely different person? The truth is that your life would look anything but familiar if you could step out of your skin and observe your routine day from the perspective of another person.

But while it's one thing to understand this conceptually, it's another thing to develop this skill and practice it on a daily basis.

Let's try a few exercises that will help us become intentional about embracing a fresh perspective. I'm confident we'll find that seeing things from the vantage point of someone else might be easier than we think!

- Stand on your front porch. Now open your front door and walk into your house and try to see it as a first-time visitor might. You might find yourself thinking things like
  —*Nice color scheme on the walls!*
  —*Wow, is that pile of mail always so high?*
  —*That overstuffed chair sure looks inviting.*
  —*Those batteries, mismatched socks, and stack of papers sure look out of place on the piano.*
- Think about how a task you're doing right now might be perceived by a child.
- Consider what life might be like for a person you pass on the street.
- What would the barista at your regular coffee shop or the delivery person at your office say to you if they felt free to speak honestly?
- Take a quantum leap for a moment and imagine a scenario in which everything changed tomorrow and you suddenly found

yourself living the life of someone else. What would you cherish most about your last day in your current life?

Do these things seem silly? Thinking outside the box, any box, is a great way to train your brain to look at your everyday experiences with fresh eyes and a new outlook.

PRACTICE APPRECIATION

When it comes to a renewed sense of wonder, appreciation changes everything. You may have come across the thought-provoking question, "What if tomorrow the only things in your life were the things you expressed gratitude for today?"

A woman who went through a season of grief and depression told me that thanking God aloud for the things she *wanted* to feel grateful for (even if her emotions were locked in the numb or sad position when she started) sparked new life in her spirit and emotions every time.

Every. Single. Time.

She said she would start out speaking with barely enough energy and motivation to mouth the words. About thirty seconds in, she would feel a shift in her spirit. Within a few minutes, joy and hope would be bubbling in her spirit.

Are you thirty seconds away from the shift you need? From going from numb, sad, bored, or resigned to feeling the bubbling of true joy and hope?

Practice appreciation. Out loud. Express gratitude to God for his blessings in your life. Say thank you to the people around you. Express appreciation to yourself for the things you do right or well.

Appreciate life.

Appreciate every minute you're given.

Appreciate others.

Be that person who loves every minute they've been given because they appreciate all they've been given. (Start this process now, and we'll talk about it in more detail throughout this book.)

PRACTICE THE PRESENCE OF GOD

You can't spend time basking in the presence of God without experiencing a shift in your perspective from the material to the eternal. When you draw near to him, you see things in a new light. His light. And it changes everything.

That thing you do every day? The mundane? The routine? The stuff that makes you yawn? That habit of yours of killing time until something seemingly more interesting happens?

Boredom? Resignation? Letting things slide? That feeling of being okay with unharnessed potential?

When you spend time with Jesus, those things are transformed into something else entirely. Purpose. Passion. Vision. Excitement. Calling. Inner peace. Intimacy. Longing for more. The empowering realization that you were created for more. That you're being equipped for more.

And everything old becomes new. Including you.

You can experience God's presence in prayer, but that's not the only activity that enhances your awareness of him. Take a walk in nature and thank him for all that he's created. Sing songs to him. Sit quietly with your eyes closed and listen for him. Invite his presence into the room where you are. Chat informally with him as you are commuting, doing chores, or taking a walk. Turn down the lights and dance with him. Start to include him in your every moment, and you will find those moments taking on supernatural significance.

Even if you're tempted to think of your days as the same ol' thing day in and day out, the truth is that every minute is new. It's unlived, unrehearsed, and unexplored.

All you need is the courage and the determination to see it. Fill your days with the childlike wonder to view the world around you as a marvel and a miracle.

FIVE

"I'LL BE THE ONE"

The first step to becoming great is being grateful.

As any parent can testify, you can learn a lot about ingratitude from a toddler. I remember an incident when my son revealed himself to be an expert on the subject.

Only three years old at the time, Max was a big fan of the cartoon character Thomas the Tank Engine. *Obsessed* might be a better word to describe his devotion. He could parrot the dialogue, sing along with the theme song, and recite all the characters' names by heart. He delighted in helping Thomas and his friends with every new task.

Now, what delighted my wife, Jen, was giving things to Max. When he asked her one day to make him a Thomas the Train costume, she poured herself wholeheartedly into the project. For an entire week she cut and painted the cardboard boxes she'd collected. The result was a perfect Thomas suit that would transform Max into his hero.

Finally, it was finished, and Jen made a plan to present the gift with maximum dramatic flair. She covered it with a sheet and brought Max into the room.

He hopped and squealed with excitement.

She ripped away the sheet with a proud flourish, awaiting squeals of delight and a profusion of praise.

Instead, Max's elated expression dissolved into a frown, and he said, "That's not the Thomas I wanted!"

Understand, his instructions had been very clear. He'd shown his mother pictures and given explicit instructions about what he wanted. When the big moment arrived, however, he'd somehow moved on and now wanted a costume resembling Percy (one of the show's other characters). Needless to say, the moment didn't go how either Jen or Max had hoped. It was spoiled by the specter of ingratitude.

Of course, a three-year-old knows nothing beyond his momentary desire and his expectation that what he wants will magically appear. His young mind was still in the process of learning that, like everything else in life, an attitude of gratitude must be cultivated and chosen again and again.

Sadly, many grown-ups seem to have never caught on to the powerful connection between gratitude and greatness. For them, life is usually much harder than it has to be. That's because the truth is, the grateful cannot fail and the ungrateful cannot succeed.

TEN WERE HEALED, ONE WAS GRATEFUL

The New Testament records a perfect example in the life of none other than Jesus Christ. Except that the kindness he granted was far, far greater than a mere favor. He saved a group of men from a horrific, deadly sickness. Their illness was so bad and so ugly that no one would go near them, not even their own families. Jesus literally gave them their lives back. But when it came time for them to say thanks, well, let's step back in time and see what happened.[1]

Jesus and his disciples had just entered a village where a cluster of ragged lepers stood off to the side, keeping their distance from a crowd who shunned them. But the teacher's reputation as a compassionate healer had gone before him, so the ten diseased men called out, "Jesus! Have mercy on us!"

He stopped and made eye contact with each one as he empathized with the unimaginable suffering these shriveled victims had endured. And in a moment of powerful grace, he said to the ten, "Go and show yourselves to the priest."

Now it's important to note that in telling the ten lepers to show themselves to the priest, Jesus was not blowing them off. Neither was he passing the buck to some other religious leader. No, the custom of the day was for the local priest to examine a once-sick person and verify that he or she was indeed well and ready to mingle again with the public.

In effect, Jesus was telling them, "I have granted your request. In the name of God and because of his power, you are healed." As the ten lepers turned and headed toward the synagogue, their blistered skin suddenly cleared, their half-eaten fingers and toes were restored, and their vitality returned. Indeed, they were healed!

THE REAL POINT OF THE STORY

This story is included in Scripture not simply to show that Jesus healed ten lepers, as remarkable as that is. The point is what happened after the gnarled men were healed. *One* of the ten returned to express gratitude to Jesus. Only one. As one translation puts it, "He couldn't thank him enough" (Luke 17:16 MSG).

But Jesus pointed out, "Were not ten healed? Where are the nine?" Then he said to the one, "Get up. On your way. Your faith has healed and saved you" (vv. 17, 19 MSG).

Ten suffering, shunned men received the blessing of healing. Their health was restored, their lives renewed. But only one of them paused, returned, and expressed thanks while the other nine went blissfully on their way.

I don't believe for a moment that Jesus inquired about the other nine because his feelings were hurt. I mean, let's be honest, we are talking about the King of kings. He was much tougher than that. Rather, his inquiry was a comment on the human condition, that our natural tendency is to grab a blessing without pausing to appreciate that blessing and give gratitude where it is due. Jesus was underscoring a key principle of successful living: gratitude and appreciation should be foremost in our thoughts, an unceasing inner attitude, a way of life not only because saying thanks is good manners but because it is crucial to experiencing God's grace and love.

It is also crucial to our own happiness and peace.

The ungrateful do not succeed in life because they are too self-absorbed, too busy, or too preoccupied to consider thoughts of appreciation. Their attitude is to ask, "What's been done for me lately?" This only makes them miserable inside and, frankly, less than pleasant to be around.

But what about those who live in gratitude, who pause to appreciate the big and little blessings of life? As we focus on the blessings and express praise, a special feeling of well-being and peace begins to flood our soul. Peace generates a knowing smile, which radiates joy, and joy honors God and uplifts those around us.

As we think about how to invest our 1440 daily minutes, I want us to learn the vital lesson of this biblical story: that our loving Creator has designed us to embrace and live out an attitude of appreciation that honors him, lifts our spirits, and also lifts those around us.

If we don't live in this way, we'll miss out on the most rewarding and enriching life that's available to us. God wants us to say, like the one man in ten, "I'll be the one to say thank you!"

If you choose to say, "I'll be the one!" just as I endeavor to do each day, you will be amazed at the positive difference this commitment brings to your life. Here are some ideas to help you get started.

LIFE IS TOUGH, BUT GOD IS GOOD

You've heard the saying, Life is good. And it often is.

But you and I both know that life can also be downright challenging. We all have good seasons and bad seasons.

That's why I prefer a revised version: "Life is tough, but God is good." That phrase acknowledges the reality that while we might feel lousy today or our circumstances just aren't pleasant at the moment, in spite of it all, God is good. Always has been, always will be. And he always has our best in mind.

I love the psalmist's admonition, "Give thanks to the LORD, for he is good; his love endures forever" (107:1). So as we grow in gratitude, let's adopt this as our underlying axiom: *Life is tough, but God is good.* This enables us to confidently give God thanks in good times as well as bad. And if another person blesses us in some way, it helps us to take notice and acknowledge the blessing with appreciation.

LOOK FOR EVERY OPPORTUNITY TO SAY THANK YOU

Being *the one* means that every time we receive a blessing, be it big or small, we turn it into an opportunity to be grateful. As we might imagine, the one healed leper returned to Jesus and leaped for joy and praised God with thanksgiving. For all the reasons we've discussed above, you and I can do the same.

Think of it this way: a blessing we receive that we *don't* turn back to praise can easily turn into *pride*. Picture what the other nine healed lepers told the priest and their friends: "Hey, *I'm* healed! Awesome, *I* don't have leprosy anymore!" Instead of placing their focus on the goodness of God, which heals, they misplaced their focus on themselves. That can lead to taking credit where credit is not due. Pride is me-centered, not God- or others-centered. And the Scriptures tell us that pride always goes before a fall (Prov. 16:18).

From this moment forward, let's turn every blessing into praise and gratitude.

OPEN YOUR EYES TO THE BLESSINGS

God's blessings are all around us every day. In fact, every 1440 minutes of each day. As we live our daily lives, we can take our eyes off ourselves and notice all the good amid the not-so-good.

Granted, it's much easier to notice *big* blessings, such as improved health, a financial boost, a new job we've been wanting, or a favor or word of encouragement from a friend. We can be aware of the smaller favors we are granted each and every day, such as:

- A roof over our head
- Blue sky
- A close friend
- Rainfall or a snowy day
- Each one-of-a-kind cloud
- The ability to move and breathe
- A job to do
- A place to sleep
- Food to eat
- The laughter of children
- An opportunity to help someone
- A walk in the woods or on the beach
- An opportunity to give
- Fresh coffee
- Sunshine

How easy would it be to breeze by these things like the other nine lepers and fail to appreciate them? But even the smallest blessings deserve praise and can bring joy. Say it with me: "I will turn every blessing back to praise. Today, I will be the one."

DON'T JUST FEEL IT—EXPRESS IT

"God, thank you for _____."

"Nancy, I sure appreciate you for _____."

"Jack, you are such a blessing to me because _____."

You can say it silently or aloud. It can be as simple as a thank you, an encouraging text, or a small gift.

The important thing is to discover the joy of being thankful and expressing gratitude early and often to the people in your life. Open your eyes, see the blessings, and express how grateful you are and why. Feel the difference inside you. See the difference among those around you.

Be the one!

SIX

MESS INTO MIRACLES

*Even on the worst day, your faith
brings transformation.*

It's always going to feel like this.

Is this your default way of thinking? It is for many of us. After all, when things are going our way, it's easy to think we've *finally* got life figured out, leaving us a little shocked and disappointed when smooth sailing turns once again into rocky seas.

And when the seas are rough? We can fall into the depressing belief that we'll never be happy again. When you're unemployed, it feels like you're *always* going to be without a job and without a paycheck. When someone you love breaks up with you, it feels like you'll *always* be lonely and miserable. When you're experiencing acute anxiety, it feels like you'll *always* be fearful and worried.

And that kind of thinking is exactly why, on our worse days, we often struggle to truly grasp the hope that is staring us in the face.

NO MESS, NO MESSAGE

We've all heard messages and testimonies in which the speaker started with a mess or went through a test, and then went on to experience blessings, provision, transformation, victory, and even miracles. "No mess, no message. No test, no testimony." We hear these stories all the time. So we know it's possible, at least for others, right?

But when it comes to our own mess or test, we close our ears and our spirits and defer back to the thought patterns that say it's always going to feel like this. We have to be open to the possibility that our mess is indeed a message for us, a story only we can live and a victory only we can grasp. Here are some ways to move your mindset from mess to message.

DO YOU REMEMBER THE LAST TIME YOU FELT LIKE THIS?

Chances are, you've gone through tough times in the past that you thought would never end. It was hard to hang on to the hope that the grief, depression, anger, hardship, or tears would ever be replaced with joy, hope, peace, and laughter. And yet that's exactly what happened.

Do you remember how relieved and maybe even surprised you felt when the clouds finally dissipated and the sun shone again?

Perhaps you can recall how profoundly grateful you felt to God in the past for bringing you through a truly dark season.

Maybe you can point to your own experience with a mess or a test that gave you a message and testimony that you share to this day.

Yet hanging on to that truth, especially as life takes you through the current or next tunnel, can feel harder than it needs to be and at times even harder than it should be. Just keep in mind that God blesses us with an unexpected gift in a season or situation we don't enjoy.

PRACTICE ACTIVE WAITING UNTIL YOUR MIRACLE SHOWS UP

It's one thing to grasp the idea that God's grace, mercy, and blessings are bigger than our biggest mess. It's a lot harder to grasp that idea emotionally.

Why? Because it usually boils down to rejecting fear and reaching for faith, and that takes intentionality. When we do these hard things and choose faith over fear, we're practicing active waiting. And active waiting sets us up for what's just around the corner from the mess, namely, *transformation*.

God uses our messes as fodder for all kinds of transformations. He might transform our circumstances. He might transform our hearts. He might transform our thinking. He might do all of these. And when our messes drive us to our knees in prayer, he will transform the way we experience him into something far more beautiful and intimate than we ever imagined.

Growing up, I never thought or imagined that my purpose and calling in life would not be purified and transformed by opportunities but instead molded by the pain of persevering through countless seasons of actively waiting.

Yes, transformation awaits. But while we're looking toward the good things God has in store for us, how do we choose faith? And not just once, but day after day while we're still living in the middle of a challenge?

Here are eight actions you can take that will empower you to make the most of every minute of even the most difficult days.

1. IMMERSE YOURSELF IN STORIES OF GOD'S FAITHFULNESS

The Bible is full of stories of messes and tests that yielded to God's relentless desire to empower and bless us. Faith, after all, comes by hearing, specifically hearing from the Word of God. Do you want to live every minute buoyed by faith as you anticipate good things ahead? Then read the inspired and inspiring stories in Scripture, starting with the accounts of Abraham, Moses, David, Mary, and John the Baptist.

2. SPEND TIME WITH REAL FRIENDS

The right friends will bolster your faith. They'll speak life into your spirit. They'll be a "tangible Jesus" to you, lifting you up, walking with you, and stirring up hope in your heart on the days you feel unable to do these things for yourself.

3. BE THANKFUL IN ADVANCE

Don't wait until your mess is transformed into a miracle to thank God for what he's going to do in your life. Live every minute in an attitude of anticipation and gratitude. You might say, "Thank you, God, in advance for carrying me through this tough season and seeing me to the other side" or "Lord, I know you will give me strength and courage to endure this painful experience, and I am thankful for your presence in my life."

4. PRACTICE GRATITUDE BEFORE SLUMBER

Our subconscious minds often linger in sleep on the last things we were thinking before dozing off. Knowing this, use the moments before falling asleep to focus on feelings of gratitude. Journal, pray, make a list. Whatever the format, focus on giving thanks before falling asleep.

5. LET ANTICIPATION GUIDE YOUR DAY

As soon as you wake up, speak positive affirmations aloud to announce to the world and to yourself what kind of good things you're anticipating in the next 1440 minutes, over the next 24 hours. You can say such things as:

"I am going to seize every opportunity to encourage the people I encounter today."

"I will use my creativity and imagination to make the world a more beautiful place."

"In the day ahead, I'll strive to be a person of grace and compassion, demonstrating God's love as best I can."

When we tell our morning brains what to anticipate and work toward, it trains us to make the most of every waking moment.

6. SOLVE A PROBLEM A DAY, EVEN IF IT ISN'T YOURS!

Don't let your current mess keep you from being a blessing in the life of someone else. Maybe you don't have the solution to your own problem today, but you undoubtedly have *a* solution to *someone's* problem. Look for a problem you can solve or at lease alleviate in the life of a friend, family member, or stranger.

Problem solving feels good. Acts of kindness feel good. Trust me, when you solve a problem for someone else, you're going to end the day feeling better than you would have if you'd simply wallowed in your own mess. The reality of our lives is this: we are either known for the problems we solve or the problems we create!

7. EXERCISE TO ELEVATE

Even when life feels messy, exercise will help you feel empowered. Exercise elevates feel-good brain chemicals like endorphins and serotonin while reducing the stress hormone cortisol. So visit the gym. Take a walk. Lift a few weights. Park in the far corner of the parking lot and walk to the entrance. Take the stairs instead of the elevator. Join a Zumba class or go for a jog. Whatever movement moves you, make it a nonnegotiable part of your day.

8. FIND POWER THROUGH PRAYER

If you're struggling to believe, ask for divine help. In the ninth chapter of Mark's Gospel, a desperate father brings his demon-possessed son to Jesus for help. When Jesus tells the father that everything is possible for the person who believes, the father cries out, "Lord, I believe; help my unbelief!" (v. 24 NKJV).

What a powerful cry for help. The truth is we can experience both faith and doubt—sometimes at the same time—and yet even on our messiest days, God is ever faithful to increase our faith when we ask him to help us.

Whatever crisis or challenge you're facing currently, your trying situation can be an opportunity for spiritual and personal growth. That's more than a feel-good pep talk. It's a reality for those who believe that God regularly turns trials into transformation and messes into miracles every minute of every day.

SEVEN

KNOW WHERE
YOU WANT TO GO

Opportunity abounds in every minute.
Be sure to use it wisely.

It was March 2000, and I had just flown into LAX to play in an important basketball tournament. Upon arrival, I rented a car, turned on the GPS, and began the hour-long drive to my hotel.

I was excited about the tournament. At that time in my life it was quite an awesome opportunity. But I was also pumped about getting to drive a vehicle with the newest technology: a portable Garmin StreetPilot GPS. Enough pumped that I had paid extra for it to be a part of the rental.

At that time, GPS technology had taken the world by storm. There had been amazing breakthroughs that everyone was eager to try. Of course that was long before today's vehicles that have GPS as a standard feature, not to mention all of the smartphones that now come with GPS preinstalled.

I was eager to get to the hotel and on to this chance to play ball, representing my team, and this device was going to help me. But the GPS in the car was in the early stages of the technology, when it was essential to frequently update the maps. If you didn't, though you might have the exact address for your destination, getting there could be a challenge.

That's exactly what happened. The rental car company had neglected to update the maps in my GPS. The Garmin was guiding me through the streets of Los Angeles, and I assumed the directions were accurate. What I didn't realize was those directions were based on an inaccurate map. Though I was in the vicinity of my hotel, I couldn't get close enough to bridge the gap between where I was and where I wanted to be. Round and round I went, frustrated at being so close and so far away at the same time!

I knew where I wanted to go, and I had the means to get there, but I was listening to the wrong directions. As a result, I nearly missed out on an incredible opportunity to participate in the tournament I'd flown in for.

That experience reminds me of something said by Leonard Ravenhill: "The opportunity of a lifetime needs to be seized during the lifetime of the opportunity."[1] In other words, don't waste precious time going around and around the wrong block and miss the opportunity to do what you're here for.

There are always going to be voices vying for your attention, shouting out possibilities for your time. Most of them would have you spend your endowment of magical minutes chasing success, which is usually defined and measured in material terms:

- Do more work in a day than most people do in a week!
- Double your income in one month!
- Score that promotion!
- Win that prize!
- Save this much by (fill in the blank) and retire in record time!

Don't misunderstand me. Those can be worthy and beneficial things to reach for. Achievement and abundance will certainly result from learning to tap the potential present in every moment, and reward naturally finds the person who seizes opportunity. But there's a subtle trap hidden in this truth that we must not ignore.

The truth is that the real aim of our search for an extraordinary life is far deeper, far richer, far more rewarding, *and* already available in the present moment. Don't listen to the wrong directions. Instead, define your outcomes wisely from the outset, and you'll save a lot of time and trouble and actually wind up where you wanted to be all along.

TO BE OR NOT TO BE

This goal, the golden opportunity to live an extraordinary life, lies in being the best possible version of yourself. That happens by fulfilling your God-given potential each and every day.

The list of characteristics below describes what that looks like. Notice that when you seize your opportunity to nurture an extraordinary life, the effect is cumulative. Each opportunity fulfilled is not an end but a miraculous opening and invitation into new levels of spiritual abundance.

What are you offered in every one of your 1440 minutes today? You have several really great opportunities.

TO BE HAPPY

What is the point of living if not to enjoy it? Yet something in our puritanical past prevents us from believing that enjoyment is an acceptable and achievable life. We've been taught that gain can only be purchased with pain. We defer the prospect of enjoying life until retirement—or for some of us maybe even the afterlife!

The truth is, perpetually postponed happiness is a recipe for disaster. Proof can be found among those celebrities who appear to have everything anyone could want but no enjoyment and no peace. All too often their stories end cruelly in burnout, addiction, and early death.

After seeing this for himself, successful actor and comedian Jim Carrey summed it up this way: "I think everybody should get rich and famous and do everything they never dreamed of so they can see that it's not the answer."[2] The answer to what? The question of what will make us happy and when.

Hear this: God not only wants you to be happy, but his desire is that joy would fuel that happiness, and he has endowed you with the perfect potential to fulfill his wish. As the psalmist told us, "You will make known to me the way of life; in Your presence is fullness of joy; in Your right hand there are pleasures forever" (16:11 NASB). Similarly, the apostle Paul wrote, "May the God of hope fill you with all joy and peace as you trust in him, so that you may overflow with hope by the power of the Holy Spirit" (Rom. 15:13).

TO BE HEALTHY

You have the power—right now, right here—to choose a lifestyle that is wholesome and healing. Your Creator has not left you at the mercy of disease and depletion. Health is your birthright. Every minute presents you with a new opportunity to step into it by taking charge of how you will nurture your body and your mind.

TO BE FRUITFUL

What does a fruitful life look like? Many would say it looks like wealth and success, that opportunity knocks for you to go after your heart's desires and possessions, but that is just one dimension of a fruitful life. Every moment is packed with the potential to harvest and store treasure in heaven.

Love, joy, peace, patience, kindness, goodness, faithfulness, gentleness, and self-control (Gal. 5:22–23). Now that's treasure! Pursue *that* potential and you'll reap the reward in every other dimension of your life as well.

TO BE FREE

Even when life feels out of control, there are things you can control. These opportunities, essentially freedoms, are available to you in every one of the 1440 minutes you have been given each day. Pursue them like treasure, because that's what they are.

- To be free of fear, guilt, shame, and anger
- To be free of the relentless sorrow that comes with toxic emotions
- To be free of any lies that bind us, body and mind, to the world's way of being
- To be free of past pain and regret and future anxiety
- To be free of all judgments, yours and those others have made against you
- To be free of people's expectations and the futile race to please them
- To be free of expectations you have placed on yourself that do not serve you

God doesn't leave us stranded or wondering how to grab hold of the freedom he offers. Cover to cover, the Bible points to the freedom found in Christ. It starts with acknowledging our brokenness and admitting we are slaves to sin. It ends with our choosing Jesus and following him daily. Only he can break the bonds of slavery and lead us to true freedom, now and forever.

Unlocking the powerful potential in each moment and using it to create a life of magnificent abundance is a lifelong journey. Like all journeys with an accurate map, it helps to know where you are going and what waits at the other end.

EIGHT

OUT OF CONTROL

To be free to let God work in you and
through you, let go of control.

I woke up in the middle of the night with a searing pain in my side. I was twenty-three and I thought I was invincible, but the severity of the pain convinced me something was seriously wrong.

I managed to drive myself to an ER. After a multitude of tests and several painful hours waiting for results, the doctors finally pinpointed the cause of the excruciating pain. Apparently I had contracted some kind of liver infection. They immediately admitted me to Durham Regional Hospital for antibiotics and fluids.

I was released a day later but remained bedridden for more than a week. I was so weak at that point I couldn't do anything for myself and had to enlist the help of friends while I slowly recovered.

Talk about an adjustment!

The change in my life took me by complete surprise. One day I was young, healthy, strong, and self-sufficient. I had the world at my feet. I had taken charge of my life, and I was going places.

An hour later I was bedridden and depending on others to help me get through the day. I was laid up, practically immobile for a week, with several more weeks until I fully recovered. Adding to the frustration, the skilled medical team never determined the cause of my infection. It just happened, causing my world to go out of control, at least temporarily.

Now when I hear those words—out of control—I don't think of *spiraling* out of control, because that's not always what we experience. I think of going to the pantry for something, say, a loaf of bread, and having every right to think it's there. After all, it was there yesterday and the day before.

But today I open the cupboard and it's bare. I didn't *spiral* out of bread; it's just gone. I had it yesterday, I thought I'd have it today, but now it's nowhere to be found.

Of course, we all want to feel in control of our lives. It's tempting to believe we know what's best for us (and maybe for others too!) and that, as long as no one gets in our way, we should take charge and try to make things turn out the way we desire.

The alternative can feel pretty scary. People can be unpredictable, and circumstances can feel random. Surrendering to the chaos of it all can feel counterproductive. How much better, we reason, to hold on to everything with a tight fist and try to muscle the pieces of our lives into position.

We want so badly to believe this is possible that we overlook the truth staring us in the face: even when we put superhuman effort into controlling our lives, we will never be fully successful.

There are few better examples than the 2020 COVID-19 crisis. Within a matter of weeks, we went from a thriving economy and life as usual to job loss, financial hardship, illness, and social isolation.

The truth is that bad things happen. Dreams are interrupted. And plans go awry. No matter how hard we try.

Utter control is not only impossible, but science tells us that our obsession with control can be detrimental. This is because people who strive the most to control their lives suffer more issues related to physical and mental health.[1] Even their relationships can suffer (do a

Google search of *how do I live with a control freak* and see how many results you get!).

In other words, our efforts to be in complete, absolute control of our lives are worse than futile. They can be counterproductive, bringing greater pain into our lives than we bargained for.

TRUE POWER LIES IN CHOOSING THE
DETAILS OF YOUR SURRENDER

This book is about owning your day and making every minute matter. But how do you make that happen when even those 1440 minutes aren't entirely in your control?

Well, I believe they are. It might seem like I'm contradicting what I just said, but hear me out. I believe we have far more control in our lives than we think we do. The problem is that our *definition* of control leads us astray.

Most of the time, when we talk about control, we're talking about controlling *outcomes*, which is a recipe for failure. We might want to control the decisions our teenager makes. We might want to control whether we will get a job offer for a sought-after position. We might want to control when a marriage proposal will come. There are simply too many variables we *can't* control. People make choices for themselves that are counter to what we want or expect. Doors of opportunity open and close. The economy triumphs and tanks ad nauseam. Even our inner struggles, conflicts, and cravings sabotage us at every turn.

No, our determination to control every outcome sets us up for failure.

And yet we really *are* in control to an extent. And the thing that remains firmly within our control is our choice: to what will we surrender?

EVERY ACT OF CONTROL IS A
CHOICE TO SURRENDER

Whenever we see people who focus on controlling everything around them, we may not immediately see the god to which they have surrendered, but we can be assured that the one God is there.

Take, for example, someone who controls a spouse through belittling words and authoritarian demands. This person may *think* they are in control, but they are deceived. In fact, every day this person is waving a white flag, having already surrendered to fears and insecurities.

Or consider the boss who tries to achieve company goals by using high-pressure, manipulative tactics with his employees. In an effort to increase productivity and performance, the driven-to-succeed boss inadvertently lowers the morale of his workforce, diminishing their enthusiasm and energy. His need for control is counterproductive, and everyone in the company ultimately loses.

The truth is, at the root of control lives fear and self-doubt.

An obsession with control is nothing but surrender to these emotions.

The good news is that if you understand this truth and choose a *different* object of your surrender, surrender can bring you everything you've ever wanted.

GOD WANTS YOU TO LOOSEN YOUR GRIP
AND PUT YOUR TRUST IN HIM

If surrender is inevitable (and it is), to what or whom will you surrender? Fear is a harsh taskmaster, as is self-doubt.

But when we surrender to God, we are submitting to an all-powerful, all-knowing, all-loving heavenly Father. And suddenly the word *surrender* takes on a whole new meaning.

When we surrender to fear or self-doubt, we are then controlled by these things.

When we surrender to God, we are set free.

Jesus promised, "Come to me, all you who are weary and burdened, and I will give you rest. Take my yoke upon you and learn from me, for I am gentle and humble in heart, and you will find rest for your souls. For my yoke is easy and my burden is light" (Matt. 11:28–30).

I imagine we all wish surrender were a once-and-done kind of thing, but it's not. Surrender is a day-by-day, even minute-by-minute kind of thing.

But it's the only way to find the power to seize your day and make every minute matter.

Our nature will always be to try to establish the illusion that we are in control of our lives. So interrupting that process means continually turning to Jesus and saying, "You've got this. I trust you."

Those words have the power to tame our unruly fears. They also diffuse self-doubt because suddenly our focus isn't on *self* at all. It's on him.

GOD WANTS YOU OUT OF CONTROL

God's plans for you are good. But in order to embrace all that he wants to do in, through, and for you, you've got to be free from the things that are holding you back.

The illusion of control is holding you back.

Fear is holding you back.

Anger is holding you back.

Perfectionism is holding you back.

Jealousy and envy are holding you back.

Greed, entitlement, and lust are holding you back.

When you let go of these things and align yourself instead with the One who holds the world in his hands, you'll find what you're looking for.

Jesus often taught in paradoxes, pairing ideas that seemed contradictory but are life changing when you understand how true they really are.

In the Sermon on the Mount in Matthew 5–7, Jesus taught that the meek, grieving, poor, and persecuted are blessed and he explained why. Later in Matthew he explained that the first will be last (19:30). He assured us that if we accept his yoke, we'll find rest (11:28–30). He promised that whoever finds their life will lose it and vice versa (10:39).

The kingdom of God has been called "the upside-down kingdom" because the way we *think* things should operate isn't the way they operate at all. In fact, true kingdom life often feels completely counterintuitive. This is why, in Isaiah 55:8, God declared, "For my thoughts are not your thoughts, neither are your ways my ways."

Giving up control for surrender can seem backward to us too. We think that gripping tighter will free us from our fears and self-doubts, but it is only by letting go and trusting Jesus that we can be truly set free. We just have to make that choice over and over; the choice is really what we have control over.

Joshua posed this challenge to the children of Israel: "Choose this day whom you will serve, whether the gods your fathers served in the region beyond the River, or the gods of the Amorites in whose land you dwell. But as for me and my house, we will serve the LORD" (Josh. 24:15 ESV).

"Choose this day."

And days are made of moments. One thousand four hundred forty of them, to be exact.

Choose well, my friend. And choose surrender over control.

NINE

NOTHING CHANGES IF NOTHING CHANGES

If we want to see something different, we need to do something different.

Mr. Brown was one of my eighth-grade teachers, and he was a big believer in the wisdom of famous quotations. He'd start every class with a new one from some of history's greats: Abraham Lincoln, Mohandas Gandhi, Eleanor Roosevelt. There was just one problem: for at least half the year he got them wrong. Every single school day for four months, Mr. Brown misquoted somebody.

My classmates and I became suspicious when the content of the quotes didn't seem to match with the person to whom Mr. Brown gave credit. It seemed fishy, for example, to think John Lennon ever made any public comments about World War I or that Winston Churchill had much to say on the subject of Broadway musicals.

But no matter how off the quotes sounded, Mr. Brown refused to believe they might be wrong, because he'd meticulously typed them all out himself. Yet even he could not remain in denial the day the quote went as follows: "There are three kinds of men. The one who learns by reading. The few who learn by observation. The rest of them have to pee on the electric fence for themselves."

With a straight face, Mr. Brown attributed this wisdom to Mother Teresa. And the class erupted in laughter.

It turned out the author of these lines was Will Rogers. The actual quote from Mother Teresa ("Intense love does not measure, it just gives") had been read the day before and attributed to Groucho Marx. Thanks to a bit of faulty word-processor formatting, the author column on Mr. Brown's sheet was misaligned, off by one line, thus throwing off the whole system.

I recalled this amusing story, and wound up laughing at myself, when I set out to begin this chapter with a famous quote by Albert Einstein: "The definition of insanity is doing the same thing over and over again and expecting different results." With a little online research I quickly discovered there's no evidence the great scientist ever said any such thing. Another lesson in being careful with quotations!

In this case, though, I think we can safely agree it's a really smart bit of wisdom, something a genius like Einstein *might* have said and then moved on.

The whole point of this book is to encourage you to believe your Creator did not make you for a life of mediocrity and to "expect different results" than those you have experienced so far. No one (you'll hear me say this again and again) can ever keep you from greatness.

At least, that's *almost* the whole truth. Because there is only one person on earth who can cause you to leave all that treasure buried in the ground.

You.

I don't think this happens because you'd rather *not* have a happier, healthier, richer, more fulfilling life. Everyone wants that! It happens because you are in the habit of spending your allotment of potential and opportunity on things that do not enrich and empower you. Your precious minutes are already full—but with all the wrong things.

OPPORTUNITY BLOCKS

Which brings us back to the insanity quote. Look closely and you'll see the wisdom in it. While faith and focused intention play a huge role in transforming your life, simply expecting different results is unlikely to get you far unless you also consider the rest of the saying and stop doing the same things over and over that have kept you stuck.

Here are some common examples.

SOCIAL MEDIA OVERLOAD

Never before in human history has a new technology emerged any faster and with more far-reaching impact than the internet. In fact, anyone who experienced lockdown during the COVID-19 pandemic (which is nearly everyone) understands just how useful online opportunities are in our society.

On the one hand, the benefits of the internet cannot be denied. Digital connectivity has transformed everything from healthcare to banking to weather forecasting. But the jury is still out as to whether some uses do more harm than good.

Social media is among this latter group. More research is needed to settle the overall question, but as a potential opportunity block, social media clearly leads the pack for lots of people. Just think of the number of our precious 1440 minutes that slip through our fingers each day while we're plugged in. Scrolling through endless postings is hypnotic, mostly fruitless, and for most of us, an undeniable waste of time.

Beyond that, people tend to cast their lives in the best possible light on social media, making it easy to believe ours is dull by comparison or, worse, a failure. When we see ourselves through that distorted lens, self-confidence wanes and potential shrivels.

Finally, mental health research has begun to document a clear link between social media exposure and an increased risk of depression and anxiety.[1] FOMO (fear of missing out) is recognized by psychologists as a legitimate source of distress for many people. But the so-called events we've become so desperate to participate in are not real in any tangible sense. That is, they do nothing to materially enhance our lives.

If you are like me, you probably have thumb twitches when you don't regularly check your Facebook, Twitter, or Instagram accounts. It's an ever-evolving world, and new apps are continually rolling out.

It's easy for us to find ourselves constantly clicking over and just thinking, *Oh, I'll check my Facebook account for any new updates for just a second.*

Who are we kidding? One little chat notification can turn into an hour-long conversation. It's a trap and a time drain. Prevent yourself from getting sucked in by setting some hard boundaries. This might mean setting time limits for your daily or weekly use of electronic devices. Or shutting down your phone and computer in the evening, well before bedtime. Or disabling the endless dings, buzzes, and vibrations that constantly pull your attention from other matters.

You will be able to get so much more out of each moment of life if you just close out your social media accounts entirely while you are actively living in the moment. You can spend time with friends face-to-face rather than just typing words to your virtual friends. You can experience the beauty of nature rather than look at digital images of it. You can feel the satisfaction of serving people in need rather than spend hours aimlessly surfing the net.

Most moments should become great memories for you and those closest to you, not memorabilia plastered online for the world to scroll through.

TOO MUCH NEWS

In principle, there's nothing wrong with being informed about the important issues affecting the world—so long as you understand that most of what passes for news is heavily slanted toward doom and gloom. Fear and outrage will always outsell hope. Spend too much time with that, and it's easy to start thinking it's game over for us all. The next step in that chain is to wonder, *Why bother imagining a better life and investing any effort in creating it?*

Anything with the power to cripple hope should be treated with extreme caution! Try going on a news diet. Fill the time you save with something more nurturing: a walk in nature, meaningful conversation, music, or even silence and contemplation. Notice the effect that has on your mental outlook.

DISTRACTING ENTERTAINMENTS

Many of the things we do to amuse ourselves have one common purpose: *to fill time*. As a defense against dreaded boredom and to avoid being alone with our tangled thoughts for long, most of us pack our minutes with empty mental calories. Like going through a bag of potato chips when you're hungry, it works for a little while, but eventually it leaves you feeling hungrier than ever.

There's nothing wrong with enjoying a night at the movies or listening to good music. Just beware of the temptation to use entertainment as a tranquilizer for your heart and mind.

TOXIC RELATIONSHIPS

It's a common misconception that to turn the other cheek means to endure mistreatment or behavior from another who in some way robs you of your God-given opportunity to thrive. It does not. It is never your job to absorb or compensate for someone else's unhappiness. Here's the danger: another person's problems can become an excuse for not reaching your own potential. What's worse, some people are quite willing to let you stay stuck there since it means they remain the center of your attention, even if for negative reasons.

The good news is, arrangements like that can't survive without your consent. Drawing new boundaries in your relationships is often a first step in building your own magnificent life. These relational boundaries might include

- saying yes to help,
- dropping the guilt and responsibility for others,
- saying thank you with no apology, regret, or shame,
- protecting your time,
- asking for space when it's needed,
- honoring what is important to you, or
- saying no to tasks you don't want to do or don't have time to do.

NUTRITIONAL DEFICITS

I hope you are beginning to see a picture emerging from all this, namely, that people can choose a lifestyle that truly works against mental health and well-being. Now let's add another dimension: *physical* depletion. The human body is very much like a high-performance automobile. Put just any old fuel in the tank and you're likely to be disappointed with the result. What you eat and drink directly determines the levels of energy and vitality available to you in the pursuit of your best life.

The science linking nutrition with overall health and well-being grows clearer every year. Here are just a few findings:

- The relative balance of bacteria in your bowels (which is heavily influenced by what you eat) has a measurable effect on your mood and mental resilience.[2]
- A diet high in trans fat, sugar, sodium, processed carbohydrates,

and meats (all the things that make fast food so tasty) triggers increased inflammation throughout the body, which is itself implicated in a host of ailments.[3]

- High-fructose corn syrup (an unexpected ingredient in many foods and beverages) produces a number of adverse health effects.[4]

Bottom line: if you are serious about seizing the power and potential for an extraordinary life that's available to you in every moment, *it matters what you eat.*

PHYSICAL STAGNATION

The health benefits of getting off the sofa or out of your chair and into motion hardly need explanation.[5] Like proper nutrition, you've heard it all before, ever since you first set foot in an elementary school gymnasium.

What you may not realize is that exercise is like a master key that helps turn the lock on all the above obstacles to great potential by delivering just the right boost in energy and motivation. There's no need to run marathons (unless that fires you up). Simply take a walk, go for a swim, play catch with the kids, ride a bike, take the stairs instead of the elevator, or do one of a hundred other things you might dream up. As simple as it sounds, the best way to get unstuck (in more ways than one) is to *move.*

CRIPPLING ADDICTIONS

As uncomfortable as it might be to talk about, we can't avoid this elephant in the room. If consuming the wrong foods can deplete your mind and body to the point of limiting your potential to thrive, what must we conclude about psychoactive drugs (legal and illicit), alcohol, and tobacco? What of other dependencies on things like gambling, shopping, sex, overeating, or pornography?

The answer is simple: addictions are a major obstacle between you and the magnificent life you seek. By definition, a compulsion pushes aside every competing desire or need until it is fulfilled. Now is the perfect time to draw a line in the sand and make every effort to get free of anything that does your thinking for you.

The truth is that addiction to anything—alcohol, drugs, gambling, pornography—is an extremely serious matter that plagues countless people. Perhaps nothing robs people of joy and contentment more than untreated addictive behavior. And nothing thwarts the potential to thrive in the 1440 minutes of each day more than addiction. If this describes you, do not let shame or stigma prevent you from pursuing the healing and well-being that God intends for you. Through his power and the resources he provides, you can achieve recovery and experience the full richness of life.[6]

FREE AT LAST

Here's the best news you've heard in a long time: *everyone* who reads this list will find room for personal improvement—starting with me!

Does that disqualify us from claiming the power and potential in the 1440 minutes God gives us each day? Does he expect you to clean house before moving on?

Never!

The point of this chapter is not to load you down with yet another burden to bear. It is to open your eyes to the vision of who you can be when you choose to reach for more than your unhelpful habits have allowed so far.

Want to be free of whatever holds you back? Every second is an opportunity to do exactly that.

TEN

CULTIVATE CONTENTMENT DURING SCARCITY

Inner peace can be yours when times are lean.

When I was growing up, my father said to me, "You can tell a lot about a person by how they treat others who can do nothing for them." In turn, I've always tried to live my life by serving others with no expectation of anything in return.

When I was a Bible college student, I volunteered to help serve a Thanksgiving dinner at an inner-city community center in Detroit. The center was in a repurposed warehouse in a neighborhood of several public housing projects and other low-income apartments. Programming during the rest of the year included, for kids, after-school art, music, and gymnastics classes and, for adults, continuing education, pro bono legal advice, and health screenings. A mobile library was parked outside one day a week.

But the Thanksgiving meal was meant for everyone, and it

seemed to me that's exactly who showed up. Nearly an hour before the advertised time, the line stretched out the door and into the parking lot. I wondered whether there was enough food to go around.

I needn't have worried. This was one of my first rodeos, but not the head cook's. I expressed my concern to her, and she smiled and calmly put me on the mashed-potato crew. When the feast began, it was my privilege to stand on the serving line and offer every single person a greeting and a helping of some delicious mashed potatoes.

By any definition, everyone I met that day was going through some heavy financial struggles. But I quickly noticed something else: some were more visibly *poor in spirit* than others: downcast, detached, disheartened. And who could blame them? Who knew what they could have been going through? I felt compassion toward and heartbroken for these suffering people, knowing most of them had experienced the kind of hardship and pain most of us never will.

As the day went on, I felt increasingly touched by those who seemed somehow broken by their circumstances. Many were reluctant to make eye contact, seemingly ashamed and afraid to be seen. Others had grown a thick armor of defensiveness, as if expecting life to land another bitter blow at any moment, and they were prepared for me to be the one who would deliver it. Whatever had happened to make them this way, it must have been terrible. It broke my heart.

While I scooped potatoes and tried to chat with them and brighten their day, I thought, *There but for the grace of God go we all. Maybe this is why Jesus so often took pity on the people who crowded around him.*

But one person at that dinner stood in sharp contrast to the others. I became aware of a young mother and her two elementary school–age kids—a boy and a girl—before they ever reached my place in the serving line. She was laughing and interacting with everyone around her. She introduced herself and her kids to the servers, whom she thanked by name and always added a warm "God bless you." Unlike some of the others, her bright eyes and irresistible smile were a nonverbal expression of joy that no one could miss. All three of them were dressed in clothes that were certainly not new, but they were clean and pressed with care. Whatever financial strain this mother was facing, she was clearly not poor in spirit.

The family moved along the line like a ray of sunshine that breaks through the clouds on a rainy day. The other people at the table where they took their seats quickly lit up with conversation and laughter. Watching from across the room, I made up my mind to speak to the woman before she left.

When they'd finished eating, I approached and introduced myself, engaging in some small talk for a minute. Then I decided to risk getting personal. I asked what made her experience of life—including the difficulty of raising two kids on her own—different from the others I had met that day.

The question seemed to surprise her, as if she'd never thought of herself in comparison to anyone else. After a moment of reflection she said, "God's not finished with us yet, and he knows what we need. That's good enough for me."

PAYING FAITH FORWARD

You might conclude this woman was extraordinary because of her positive attitude in the midst of hardship. Technically, you'd be right, but she had chosen to actually *exercise* a power that belongs to each and every one of us. That is, the ability to choose how we interpret and experience what happens to us one moment at a time.

The truth is, having little in the way of money or possessions is not the best definition of poverty. Embracing and internalizing the role of the victim and acting accordingly is, however.

Don't misunderstand what I'm trying to say. It's not my intention to judge anyone or to trivialize the painful path they have walked.

Who am I to say I would have responded any differently had I endured the pain and trauma they have endured?

But that woman's aura of joy suggested to me that each of us *can* respond differently if we choose to do so with faith, hope, trust, and love. If you find yourself in the middle of this battle today, it can help to remember a few fundamental facts.

LIFE MOVES IN SEASONS AND CYCLES

There was a time, not very long ago by historic standards, when everyone arranged their lives around the natural rhythms and cycles of the earth: the seasons, the weather patterns, the rising and setting of the sun. Their livelihoods depended on knowing their place in the natural dance and moving with it, not against it.

Today, in urban environments that never sleep, artificially controlled by technology, it's possible to believe we've risen above that. But this is an illusion that cannot change an unassailable fact: from the cosmos to the cornfields, everything moves and shifts according to God's rhythm—rising and falling, growing and dying, assembling and dissolving. Every end is a beginning and vice versa.

That means wherever you find yourself in the story of your life, you can be sure it is not the last page. "God is not finished with us yet," my Thanksgiving dinner friend said. She understood there is always hope while we're alive. To forget that is to deny the very nature of God's divine sovereignty in the world.

RESISTANCE IS THE ROOT OF DISCONTENT

One of the hardest and unhappiest things I ever did as a child was household chores. Don't get me wrong. I was no Cinderella, forced to work from dawn to dusk. Compared with my parents, my share of the load was light. The problem and the source of my distress was not the work itself. It was how hard I fought against doing it. It took years for me to understand that my mother was right, week after week, when she said, "You're spending way more energy trying to get out of it than it would cost to just do the job!"

Some people mistakenly see the practice of contentment in tough times as a spiritually enlightened sacrifice we make for God's benefit. Not so! In surrender to what is, *we're* the ones who gain. Embrace where you are even as you pray and work for relief. Let go of the struggle and you'll find the pathway to receiving a priceless promise: "And the peace of God, which transcends all understanding, will guard your hearts and your minds in Christ Jesus" (Phil. 4:7).

HARDSHIP ALWAYS HAS A GIFT FOR YOU

When the COVID-19 pandemic arose in early 2020, millions of Americans lost their jobs overnight. Many had positions they had considered bulletproof against ordinary economic uncertainty. My friend Janae was one of them when she, like so many, was suddenly unemployed.

"In no time I went from shopping online for vacation destinations to searching for the nearest food pantry," she said. With schools and daycare centers closed, her two boys had nowhere else to be but home.

Initially, Janae felt waves of panic and grief at all she had lost and with no certainty it would ever return. Then something miraculous happened. Unable to take the kids out to eat as she often did before, she noticed how much she enjoyed cooking meals at home. The food was healthier, and the time she spent with the boys was more satisfying. To-do projects she'd put off for months were now done. She reached out to family and friends whom she'd long neglected in the hustle of her busy schedule. The more she looked, the more she found areas of life that were *better* than before the pandemic struck.

For many months the financial hardship was real and frightening, but the gift in it was this: When her boss eventually invited her back to work, Janae resolved to hang on to the unexpectedly positive life changes she had made in her season of hardship. When money and security were in short supply, joy and contentment emerged in abundance.

WHAT YOU THINK AND SAY, YOU CREATE

It's natural to have thoughts and worries about what we lack, but when we focus on that lack and who we think we are as a result of it, it can be visible in the way we engage with others.

So many of us with the Western worldview treat life as something that happens *to* us through external conditions and forces beyond our control. Our thoughts are simply a response to circumstance, mostly in the form of observation and commentary, but with little creative power of their own. In a later chapter, I'll discuss in detail why this is untrue and what causes us to miss out on an enormous opportunity to thrive. For now, let's just acknowledge that negative self-talk and visualization—that constant inner dialogue that seems to point out everything that has gone wrong (or soon will)—is not just a drain on your emotional immune system, but it literally helps to create the very conditions it fears.

When you tell yourself first thing in the morning that it's going to be a lousy day, it most likely will be.

When you envision yourself failing at the big work presentation, it's probably not going to be your shining moment.

When you expect the next family reunion to be full of tension and drama (like the last one), you just might find yourself in a contentious situation.

To avoid the poverty trap, choose your thoughts and your words carefully!

GRATITUDE IS TIMELESS

It's a little-known fact you cannot think two thoughts at the same time. Try it and you'll see. So one way to take charge of your negative thoughts is to replace them with gratitude. If you're serious about honestly looking, you'll never lack for things to be grateful for: food, shelter, friends, family, music, intelligence, health. The list could go on.

But consider this powerful twist: try being grateful for the things *you don't yet have*.

Just after telling his disciples they could move mountains with a command, Jesus said, "Therefore I tell you, whatever you ask for in prayer, believe that you have received it, and it will be yours" (Mark 11:24). What better way to train yourself to believe your prayers are answered than to give thanks in advance?

Chances are we'll all face lean seasons from time to time. But never believe the opportunity for inner peace is dead and buried. It can be achieved when you have little just as much as during times of plenty. You can echo the powerful words of the apostle Paul: "I have learned to be content whatever the circumstances. I know what it is to be in need, and I know what it is to have plenty. I have learned the secret of being content in any and every situation, whether well fed or hungry, whether living in plenty or in want" (Phil. 4:11–12).

Nurture a sense of gladness and fulfillment throughout the minutes of this day and every day. And like my Thanksgiving friend and my suddenly unemployed friend Janae, you might find yourself bringing light and hope to everyone around you, even in hard times.

ELEVEN

KEEP PERSPECTIVE THROUGH PLENTY

*The heart is revealed in your response
to blessing and success.*

Ebenezer Scrooge.

I guarantee, without saying another word, your mind has already filled with the image planted there by Charles Dickens in his classic novel *A Christmas Carol*. Close your eyes and see a mean, shriveled old miser who values profit over people and even over his own welfare. He denies himself the warmth of an extra brick of coal just as much as he denies it to his clerk, Bob Cratchit. It's fair to say that Scrooge is wretchedly wealthy.

The theme of Dickens' cautionary tale—money corrupts—has been repeated so often now, in so many stories, we hardly question it. So it is wise to pause for a moment and consider that idea with fresh eyes.

Is it true that Scrooge is wretchedly wealthy? Or is he wretchedly *unhappy* in spite of his wealth?

That's an important distinction.

HOW WE THINK AFFECTS WHO WE ARE

Lots of well-meaning people conclude that money is intrinsically evil. They try to sanctify poverty as somehow morally superior to abundance or to vilify people who are well off. I humbly suggest that's a mistake. Don't miss a golden opportunity to grow and to claim the extraordinary nugget of wisdom God wants us to see through this story.

As *A Christmas Carol* demonstrates, it is Scrooge's mental and spiritual *relationship* with his wealth that causes the trouble, not money itself. Precisely the same thing can be said of people who have too little in the way of material riches *and* are just as bitterly unhappy.

At both ends of the spectrum it is how we *think* about wealth that affects who we are and how we experience life, including the 1440 minutes that comprise this day. So how do we do that?

Fortunately, God gave each of us exactly what we need to escape Scrooge's fate. To integrate material well-being into a happy, healthy, and magnificent life, we need to use the power of *choice*. You get to decide what to think and therefore to determine your own relationship with money at any level. Here are five proven ways to do that.

BE GRATEFUL

There's a reason gratefulness plays a part in almost every discussion we've had so far. And it's no less powerful in this case.

Nothing beats the practice of *radical* gratitude for helping us to maintain the proper perspective in the midst of plenty. I call it radical because it goes far beyond most people's typical thanks at mealtimes or once a week at church. I'm talking about cultivating a constant awareness of a deep and transformative truth: *everything* is a gift from God, including all you have earned through your labor.

The late astronomer and philosopher Carl Sagan captured this truth in the following: "If you wish to make an apple pie from scratch, you must first invent the universe."[1] In other words, everything we do depends on all that God is and does for us.

It's remarkably common for people who've been blessed with wealth (or talent or favorable circumstances or serendipitous timing) to get the idea that *they* are their own source of good fortune. "I got where I am by hard work, sacrifice, and willpower," they say. That certainly describes the way Scrooge saw himself. But to call ourselves providers without gratitude for *God's* prior provision is to misunderstand the very nature of existence.

Radical gratitude short-circuits this error before it can develop. Saying "thank you" as often as possible reminds you that every minute is jam-packed with blessings that come to you as freely as the air you breathe or the sun that warms you.

BE HUMBLE

How do times of plenty affect our relationships with others?

God did not create the universe (and make apple pie possible) for a select few, for only those willing and able to do what it takes to succeed. The Bible makes it plain that the rain falls equally on everyone, and seeds germinate the same way no matter who plants them (Matt. 5:45).

And yet so often our materialistic culture tells us the wealthy are somehow entitled to privilege and prestige that others don't deserve. At best this fosters a disregard for others and, at worst, the kind of cruel exploitation Dickens wrote about so passionately.

It's true that having money grants you access to a wider range of experiences and possessions. It opens some doors that are closed to the poor. But what it never, ever does is convey greater human *worth* on those who have it.

When opportunity favors you with fruitfulness, be careful to remember that all God's children are equal in his eyes.

BE GENEROUS

Gratitude and humility are stepping-stones to the next level of perspective in the midst of plenty: *generosity*. This might not surprise you. Those who have been especially blessed often feel the need to give back. Lots of people check that box with charitable donations at the end of every year.

Still, we can do better.

In *A Christmas Carol*, suppose Scrooge had responded to his harrowing night with the spirits by simply buying the prize goose for the Cratchits' Christmas dinner and calling it done. No raise for Bob the following day. No extra coal for the stove. No medical help for Tiny Tim. No change at all in how he conducted his business or his life the rest of the year.

I suspect that if Dickens had written *that* ending, none of us would know anything about his story today because it would have been unsatisfying and easily forgettable. The story *is* beloved because it calls us to a much higher standard, to adopt love and generosity as a *way of being*, not just an occasional action.

Real giving is more than sharing a few dollars. It's about using one's resources to ignite hope in others and to fan the flames with sustained empathy and compassion. That doesn't always mean launching a new nonprofit. Every kind word, every warm smile, every genuine connection and small need met is an act of real generosity.

BE PRESENT

Your ability to be *here now* is a key that unlocks the extraordinary life you are meant to live.

Paradoxically, wealth can make this harder to achieve and sustain. That's because once you have money, it's natural to want to protect it, invest it, and grow it. As wise as those goals are, they also pose a danger to your enjoyment of each moment. In order to succeed, you focus attention in the future, analyze your prospects, anticipate possible threats, and weigh appropriate responses. It comes with the territory. But if you are not careful, prudence can quickly become preoccupation, and then full-blown anxiety.

That will always make you less available to new waves of opportunity to truly *enjoy* the life you've worked to create, to authentically connect with the people around you, and to tend to self-care along the way.

Be sure your money serves you and not the other way around by keeping your mind where it belongs—in the now.

BE TRUE

Military leaders are taught to be on guard against something called mission creep, that is, the danger the original purpose of an operation will gradually shift over time in increments so small that the change escapes notice. For instance, a humanitarian mission to deliver food to people suffering from famine can slowly morph into combat patrols to stop bandits from stealing the food. That doesn't happen overnight but through several seemingly tiny decisions over time.

While that's an extreme example, the same thing can happen with material prosperity. What started off as a healthy desire to fund your best life according to your own principles, to provide greater comfort and security for your family and have surplus to share, can subtly drift to the point where amassing and maintaining wealth becomes its own objective. A compromise here and a shortcut there leads to a new way of being that you no longer recognize and would never have signed up for in the beginning.

The solution is to be crystal clear about the values you hold, to make a fierce commitment to continue to hold them, no matter what, and to process every decision with your personal mission statement in mind.

Material abundance is not a harvest to seek for its own sake; it is *fertilizer* meant to nourish something much better, namely, your emerging life of extraordinary power and purpose.

TWELVE

TO MOVE
BEYOND, LEAVE
IT BEHIND

*Focus not on who you were but on
who you are becoming.*

I met Martin when we were seated next to each other on a long flight across the country. It was the middle of the night, a true red-eye express. The plane was packed but mostly dark and quiet. Here and there overhead lights marked the passengers who were catching up on work or passing the time with a book or on their phone.

Before takeoff, Martin and I had the usual small talk. I learned he had just turned thirty and was a recording engineer who owned his own studio. He had already produced several promising artists.

I've come to expect one of two general reactions when I share *my* profession. The revelation that I'm a pastor either stops the conversation in its tracks because people fear being on the receiving end of a sermon, or it makes them jump at the chance to talk with someone safe about something that's bothered them. Martin fell into the latter camp.

"Can I ask you a question?" he began.

"Of course, if I can have your permission to give an honest answer, not just one you might want to hear," I replied.

He paused to consider that and then agreed.

"Is it possible for your soul to be mortally wounded while your body keeps on living?"

It was my turn to pause. His question had depth that was anything but typical. Only someone in real pain could ask it. I silently trusted God for the wisest possible response and knew the best way to start was by listening.

Martin had been fascinated with sound since he was a boy. While in high school he built a rudimentary studio in his parents' basement and began doing sessions for friends who were musicians. A few of his recordings even sold well locally and garnered the type of underground success that built a pretty crazy fan base. Even then, he still thought of engineering as a hobby.

Then he met Megan.

"She didn't do music, she *was* music," Martin recalled. "In just one session she challenged me to be more than I thought was possible, to be a true sound *artist*."

He took that to heart and helped produce her first EP, which propelled her significantly as an up-and-coming singer-songwriter. With her encouragement, he became serious about his education and launched into a career in audio production. Along the way Martin and Megan fell in love and were married. It was a perfect match.

"Nobody ever had it better than I did," he told me.

Then, just when Megan's music was poised to take a national stage, she was diagnosed with breast cancer. She died within a year. Martin was twenty-eight at the time.

The plane's engines droned in the background, and we were surrounded by dozens of people, but as he told his story we might as well have been the only two people on earth.

"I think my soul is in a coma or something," he said. "I'm here and not here at the same time."

Finally, it came time for me to try to answer his question. He was looking for hope that healing was possible after such a grievous loss and perhaps to understand why it had happened in the first place. His eyes were dry, but tears had welled in mine. Drying them away, I told him I had learned two very important things in my life: there is a God and I'm not him.

I have no idea why beautiful people who are gifted and full of life die so young. I don't understand why innocent people are victimized or abused or why wars rage or hunger persists.

What I *do* know is that we have a Creator who loves us beyond anything we can ever imagine. Nothing is beyond his healing grace.

Ever.

CROSSING THE EVENT HORIZON TO FREEDOM

Trauma like Martin's can feel like a black hole, with gravity so strong nothing can escape, not even light. In a real black hole, physicists call the point of no return the *event horizon*, a boundary that divides our vibrant universe from the crushing darkness beyond. I think it's an apt description of emotional and spiritual trauma as well.

An event in the past opens a deep well of pain, regret, guilt, shame, grief, anger, rage, or jealousy. But there is always a threshold in our mounting distress where it seems we might lose ourselves and fall in for good. One thing determines whether we keep sinking or make our way back to healing, and it's often something we'd rather not face. (It's also the reason I asked for Martin's permission to give an *honest* answer and not necessarily a comfortable one.) The event horizon when dealing with past trauma is this: the decision to *let it go*.

I know. The idea of letting go goes against instinct, experience, cultural norms, and well-meaning advice. To let go of past wounds seems wrong to us, as if it dishonors the one we lost or exonerates the one who harmed us or invites history to repeat itself. None of that is true. But nothing can extract us from the past as long as we hang on to it for dear life.

Of course, that's easy to *say*. To make it work in the real world, there are six practical tools that will help.

REFRAME YOUR PAIN

Throughout this book we've been talking about reaching for the extraordinary potential in every moment. It's easy to think this kind of opportunity is only found in sunlit pastures flowing with milk and honey. Sometimes it is, and we gratefully meet it there.

But there's no denying that *hardship* can also open doors to personal evolution and expansion that might otherwise remain stubbornly closed. That doesn't make it hurt less, but knowing it can draw you back from the edge of despair.

RELEASE THE URGE TO BLAME

Judgment is a thick chain that binds you to the past. Why? Because to maintain a sense of righteous outrage (or shame, if the person you have to blame is yourself), you've got to keep the event fresh in your mind, in vivid detail. The result is like the plot of a bad Hollywood thriller: you are doomed to repeat the painful memory over and over.

There is only one way out: *forgiveness.*

This doesn't come naturally to anyone, mostly because we mistakenly think forgiving is the same thing as forgetting. We balk at letting someone off the hook for something we feel should never have happened.

The truth is, it did happen. Nothing will change that. But until you let go of the need to find fault, the only person still on the hook is you.

RETHINK YOUR SEARCH FOR ANSWERS

There's a one-word question at the heart of most unresolved past trauma: why? And it is a bottomless pit.

Martin wondered why God would allow the woman he loved to be taken by cancer. But he tortured himself even more with another, more personal version of the question. He told me he sensed something was not right with Megan months before her diagnosis, but he didn't say anything out of fear and denial.

"*Why* did I do that?"

Only God knows the answers to such haunting questions, and he also knows exactly what you need in order to heal. Asking the painful and perplexing why questions is normal and natural. It's a part of being human. And God accepts our questions. To be free of the past, trust him with your why thoughts and words, and believe his answers and his ways are always reliable.

REINFORCE YOUR POWER

Past trauma can feel like kryptonite (the alien substance that saps Superman's strength and leaves him at the mercy of his enemies). In our case, however, the thing that drains us is not a mysterious mineral; it's a word, an idea that takes root in our minds and traps us in the past: *victim*.

The dictionary defines victim simply as "someone harmed by an unpleasant event."[1] That may be technically true about you. But when you wrap yourself in that identity like a cloak, it takes on a deeper, more destructive meaning. A sampling of synonyms tells the story: dupe, chump, easy target, laughingstock, patsy, fool. Start thinking of yourself in those terms and you'll feel hope slipping away.

Whatever happened to you in the past, choose empowering words to describe yourself now as you work toward healing. You might use words such as *survivor* or *overcomer* or *victor* or *conqueror* or another word that exemplifies your strength and resilience.

RETURN YOUR AWARENESS TO THE PRESENT

Here's a bold statement that is nonetheless true: preoccupation with the past is delusional, that is, it causes you to spend precious time living in a reality that no longer exists except in your mind. Like any daydream, the past is a hypnotic trance that robs you of lucid awareness in the here and now.

Pay attention when you are wandering in your memories, and purposely place your thoughts on what is right in front of you at this moment. Practice mindfulness, which encourages you to focus on your breathing and senses. Concentrate on the sights and sounds of the space around you, pick up objects and run your hands over them. Turn your full attention to any people you're with, savor each sip of your coffee, feel the weight of your body, and take notice of the feelings you experience moment by moment.

REIMAGINE THE FUTURE

Much of what makes past trauma so painful is how it alters the future you thought you could count on. Afterward, the world looks different because *you* are different for having experienced an upheaval of some kind.

The process of letting go includes releasing your previous vision of the future and replacing it with a more empowered version of your choosing. The days and years ahead may not be what you hoped for or expected, but the different and new version of the future you anticipate can bring you unexpected opportunities to grow and thrive.

Is the "future you" broken or handicapped by the past? Or are you stronger, wiser, and more resilient? You get to decide. In this way, choosing a new vision for your future is not mere reverie or wishful thinking but an intentional process of renewing your hope and refreshing your expectation for the life you are stepping toward.

Don't let past pain rob you of present opportunities. Now truly is all you have, but there is nothing more you could ever need. This moment—and *only* this moment—is unspeakably rich with power and potential for the abundant life God promised you.

THIRTEEN

MASTER THE MOMENT

If you can learn to maximize your thoughts, you will maximize the power in every minute.

I'll never forget going to Barnum & Bailey's three-ring circus on a field trip with my school, Christian Faith Center Academy, when I was ten. In addition to the vivid colors and beautiful chaos, I was fascinated by the animals.

I especially loved the opening parade.

As the massive elephants, Clydesdale horses, and lions thudded, pranced, and stalked their way around the rings beneath the spotlights, I couldn't tear my eyes away. I was amazed that the animals didn't fight or attack each other. They didn't even wander out of the line. In fact, they never missed a step, but moved in sync with one another.

Although these animals were massive, and some were capable of great destruction, a single man, the ringmaster, was guiding them all. And good thing he was! If even one of the animals had refused to come under the leadership of the ringmaster, there would have been a huge animal pileup. Anything could have happened.

The ringmaster seemed fully aware of what each animal was up to. Sometimes he signaled for one animal or another to speed up or slow down. He kept them all on pace, and he controlled that pace.

I remember thinking, *This ringmaster has really figured out how to make these animals do exactly what he wants them to do and at the exact right time.*

At the time I was too young to realize that as soon as I learned to embrace this concept and apply it to my own thoughts and attitudes, it would have the power to change my life.

Of course, learning how to be the ringmaster of our thoughts doesn't happen overnight. It takes time and practice.

Sometimes we have to catch ourselves in the act of failing, and then make the decision to take charge of our thoughts, despite frustrating circumstances, to really begin to own this powerful principle.

It reminds me of a parking lot experience at a local grocery store.

I had just pulled into the lot, hoping to get in and out of the store quickly. I'd had a long, frustrating day, and I wanted to make short work of the list my wife, Jen, had texted to me as I left the office for the day.

That didn't happen. In fact, I couldn't even *park* quickly. You know the drill: cars crawling up and down in search of the best spot, harried people pushing carts in every direction, a store employee gathering empty carts in a long line that backed up traffic, the call and response of frustrated honking.

I could only imagine what the lines were like inside the store.

Looking back, I realized the hectic scene was a lot like my mind that afternoon. My thoughts were far away, back in the church conference room where I'd had meeting after meeting earlier in the day. In truth, this parking lot traffic jam was just one in a series of frustrating things I had encountered that week, and I was feeling a little sorry for myself.

If I'm totally honest, I was feeling more than a *little* sorry for myself.

I was thinking, *People can be so stupid!* and *I deserve better than this.* To top it off I had a commitment that evening that I dreaded but saw no way to avoid.

This day is shot. Why am I even here? I deserve to be home relaxing. I have every right to be frustrated and annoyed right now.

I inched my way through the parking lot, feeling irritated with the guy pushing his cart down the middle of the lane. Finally, he veered off and I saw a car readying to back out.

Eager to grab the spot, I pulled forward and nearly smacked the rear end of a station wagon that abruptly backed out in front of me.

Irritated, I put my car in reverse and backed up to give the wagon more room. Then, before the lumbering battleship drove away, I saw it. And it was exactly what I needed to see at that moment.

On the back window of that annoying wagon was a faded, peeling bumper sticker.

Don't believe everything you think.

If someone had suddenly appeared and slapped that sticker on *my* windshield, the effect could hardly have been more dramatic. Instantly, I mentally downloaded this simple message. I got it and suddenly felt embarrassed and regretful about how preoccupied I'd been, to the point of being downright unfriendly, all because I was letting my thoughts run away with me.

I *believed* the cranky, self-absorbed commentary my mind was feeding me.

I, like nearly everyone, have always considered my thoughts to be mostly an automatic function of being alive, like breathing and digesting. Something happens and I respond with a thought about it. Rinse and repeat all day long. Then, along comes a bumper sticker to suggest I could (and should) have a different relationship with my thoughts, one in which I am in charge for a change.

Step one, I realized, was simply to be aware of my thoughts—*all* of them.

BE YOUR OWN RINGMASTER

Is it really possible for the mind to become aware of its own process of thinking? Absolutely!

That doesn't mean it's easy. It takes determination and discipline to disrupt the habitual flow of your thoughts in order to see what's really going on in there. Anyone can do it, but you have to want to enough to stay at it.

So what's the payoff? The fact is, left unchecked, your mind will spend most of its time thinking about the past (my terrible week) or the future (the evening I wanted but couldn't have). We relive past traumas and failures while worrying about future uncertainties and obligations.

All. The. Time.

If your goal is to capitalize on every one of the 1440 minutes God gives you today, then time spent chasing your thoughts through the past as well as the future is time wasted. Thankfully, it is possible to stop believing the parade of thoughts about things that don't exist in the present. Here's how.

OBSERVE

Here is a counterintuitive and maybe even startling truth: *you are not your thoughts.* That's a little hard to grasp at first because, as I've pointed out, most of us identify completely with everything going on in our heads. It's reflected in our language. I say, "I *am* angry" or "I *am* sad" or "I *am* happy." The "I" we are referring to is the collection of past memories, present preferences, and future dreams we've amassed, that is, our thoughts.

To see why this is misleading, try this simple experiment. Find a quiet place where you can be undisturbed for a few minutes. Make yourself comfortable. Take a few deep breaths to settle into the moment. Now spend a little time noticing your thoughts. Don't judge them, fight them, or force them in a particular direction. Just observe what pops up. What to have for dinner. The phone call you owe your sister. Reasons why it is stupid to sit and observe your thoughts.

Once you've done that for a few moments, ask yourself, *If my mind was thinking those things, who was the one observing just now?* That's the real you, made in God's image and able to do far more than spectate. It's the you who can learn to exercise the power of intentional thought to create a better life than you've imagined.

This is what I like to call *mindfulness*, a practice that helps people tame runaway thoughts, calm anxiety, and keep problems in perspective.

FEEL

Sometimes your mind is too chaotic to stand still for simple observation. That's when *thinking* may not be the best tool for untangling your thoughts. Fortunately, you have another clue that can help: your *emotions*.

When it's especially difficult to answer the question, "What am I thinking right now?" shifting attention to what you *feel* can bring clarity. That day in the parking lot, it might have been easier for me to notice that my feelings were out of joint and wonder what thoughts had led me there, rather than to sort out my thoughts directly.

If I had, then the observer in me could have chosen new thoughts that felt better, such as gratitude in place of self-pity or compassion rather than anger. Or I might have asked for God's blessing on the people whom I perceived as annoying. Identifying our feelings leads to thoughts we can consciously choose to shift from negative to positive, from destructive to constructive.

QUESTION

When you've observed your thoughts and feelings and recognized they are not your real identity, it's time to analyze them with three powerful queries.

1. Is this thought really mine?

That may seem odd, since you just observed it happening in your own mind. But the truth is, our minds are filled with thoughts that didn't originate there. We inherit them from our parents, siblings, teachers, coworkers, advertisers, politicians, writers, whoever's around us. Like viruses, thoughts are easily transmissible.

Suppose you observed this recurring thought: *I am incapable of succeeding. I never finish what I start.* Is that truly what *you* believe? Or if you listen more carefully, do you hear someone else's voice from long ago telling you that until you believed it and made it your own?

2. Is this thought really true?

No matter how you answer question 1, it's important to keep going. Perhaps it *is* true you've had trouble committing to things, but the good news in seeing that is now you can make a different choice going forward.

On the other hand, you may discover the thought you've carried around for years is a complete lie. *I'm unattractive, and no one will ever want me* is a sadly common example.

You may be surprised to find that your mind has been plagued for years by thoughts that are neither yours nor true.

3. Is this thought helpful?

Assuming your goal is to make the most of every one of the 1440 golden opportunities you were given today, why would you waste time on a thought that keeps you trapped in mediocrity and malaise? Whatever else you may have discovered about a thought, if it is not helping you to be your best self, then it has to go!

CHOOSE

That brings us to the last tool in the box: your ability to decide for yourself what to think and feel and to refuse to play the mind's games that no longer serve you.

With this power, you can choose to align your thoughts with God's thoughts. How? By realizing that everything he ever thinks comes from the same place: *love*.

The apostle Paul wrote:

Love is patient and kind; love does not envy or boast; it is not arrogant or rude. It does not insist on its own way; it is not irritable or resentful; it does not rejoice at wrongdoing, but rejoices with the truth. Love bears all things, believes all things, hopes all things, endures all things. Love never ends. (1 Cor. 13:4–8 ESV)

You can't go wrong when you choose love. Use it as a filter for your thoughts and feelings but also as an indicator for when those things are in need of alignment. It really is your choice.

Mastering one's thoughts through awareness and loving intention is not the default setting, and it's often not easy. As with any skill it takes practice. But you'll never be sorry. It's a huge step in the journey into a magnificent life beyond merely existing.

FOURTEEN

REST TO GIVE YOUR BEST

As much as we'd like to be superhuman,
God made us to need rest.

Endurance. Extreme sacrifice. Single-minded discipline. Amazing achievement in the face of insurmountable odds. These all sound pretty admirable, right?

Our culture honors entrepreneurs who eat nothing but ramen noodles for years while launching their business, athletes who give up every other pursuit to push their bodies and minds beyond the breaking point, adventurers who risk everything to conquer the next challenge. We applaud the grit of someone who scorns any suggestion of self-care.

"I'll sleep when I'm dead!" they scoff.

It makes for a thrilling story. But is it a realistic way to be? Is it *wise*? Perhaps some people are hardwired to live on the edge of endurance and are endowed with the stamina to thrive there. But what about the rest of us?

One possible downside of our admiration of extreme achievement is that it encourages us to believe it's the *only* way to get what we want in life. "No pain, no gain." This keeps many people frozen in the starting blocks, afraid to chase their dreams, knowing they can't live up to this standard. That, in turn, leads to feelings of inadequacy and failure. Unable to match such intensity, they conclude something must be wrong with them.

But it's not. Treating ourselves this way runs contrary to what science tells us about the needs of the human body and mind. Research has confirmed again and again that rest is a key component of what it takes to be healthy.

For example, the benefits of simply getting a good night's sleep include:

- Better productivity and concentration
- Lower risk of obesity
- Lower risk of heart disease and stroke
- Better athletic performance
- Greater emotional and psychological resilience
- Lower inflammation
- Stronger immune function[1]

The bottom line is, chronic depletion and stress from lack of rest are a recipe for disaster. God created human beings to need ample time each day for regeneration. For the vast majority, living our best, most abundant life simply isn't possible without it.

HAMSTERS ON A WHEEL

Our cultural infatuation with extreme achievement isn't the only thing that keeps us chasing our tails these days. There are other, perhaps even deeper reasons most people find it so hard to relax and rest. Here are a few of them.

WE'RE AFRAID OF WHAT HAPPENS IF WE STOP RUNNING

Many people live paycheck to paycheck, with a thin margin for financial error. Constant anxiety drives them to do whatever it takes to stay one step ahead of catastrophe. That means attempting to anticipate every threat and cover every contingency. It's exhausting! But once you believe this is what it takes to survive, the notion of self-care—relaxation, ample sleep, accepting help from others, and sharing your feelings—sounds like a luxury you can't afford.

But it would be a mistake to say this condition only afflicts poor people. Material resources are no guarantee you'll be free from fear. In fact, there's plenty of evidence that wealthy people can be just as anxious about the future as anyone, perhaps even more. The constant need to monitor interest rates, stay on top of stock markets, watch trends in property prices, and so on is no small burden.

Whatever your financial status, hyperactive vigilance is costly to well-being.

WE'RE CHASING SOMEONE'S APPROVAL

Lots of people work harder than necessary in the hope they can finally prove their worth to someone whose opinion they value. It doesn't matter whether the other person's disapproval is real or only imagined. The pressure it creates to excel and achieve, no matter the cost, can be intense. Those goals are also likely to be a moving target, since what it takes to secure someone's blessing today may change next week.

Under those conditions, slowing down seems to threaten our most basic need for acceptance and belonging. It's no wonder we keep striving.

WE'VE MISTAKEN WHAT WE DO FOR WHO WE ARE

In this case it's not about how others see you but about how you see yourself. If you've staked your sense of identity on whether you succeed or fail at something, you're unlikely to make rest a high priority. The consequences of failure are simply too severe. Much of the time your identity includes not only what you do but how well you do it. You're driven not only to outperform others but also yourself, year after year. If you don't, you wonder, who will you *be?*

The tragic trap in this way of thinking is that exhaustion and burnout are the fastest ways to fail at anything you set out to do or be.

WE'RE ADDICTED TO HYPERACTIVITY

The truth is, many people have never known any other way to live. They stepped into the fast lane as children, with one project or activity piled on another, and then carried all of that into adulthood. Chances are that has opened the door to all the reasons for restlessness listed above. But now they must also deal with a powerful consequence: *habits.*

Like any addict, a person addicted to activity may panic when the object of their dependency is threatened—in this case, frantic busyness—and will do anything to defend it. A telltale sign of this condition is a deep fear of being bored and a never-ending need to fill every moment with something.

A NEW WAY OF BEING

Given all that, it's understandable when people think making the most of opportunity in every moment means *working harder than ever.* Understandable but quite untrue! God has provided a different way. He gives us a miraculous path out of the maze of overwork and exhaustion in a timeless and liberating concept: *sabbath.*

In modern times, the word *sabbath* has been limited to vaguely refer to Sunday, and only because that's the day when weekly church services are held. In truth, God designed the sabbath to be so much more than that, not for his benefit, but for ours.

The practice of treating a sabbath day differently is meant to remind us of our need for rest. After all, the Genesis story says God himself rested from the labor of creation. But the real power of the sabbath lies in what it suggests about our relationship to God the other six days as well. It is an exercise, above all, in surrender to something other than ourselves as the source of survival and abundance. Once you grasp that, it's impossible to limit the freedom it conveys to a single day.

Here are the traits you need to "remember the Sabbath day, to keep it holy" (Ex. 20:8 ESV).

TRUST

Jesus summed up the essence of living the sabbath mindset in this way:

> Therefore do not be anxious, saying, "What shall we eat?" or "What shall we drink?" or "What shall we wear?" For the Gentiles seek after all these things, and your heavenly Father knows that you need them all. But seek first the kingdom of God and his righteousness, and all these things will be added to you. (Matt. 6:31–33 ESV)

At the heart of all frantic scrambling to provide for yourself or achieve what you've set out to do is the belief that your life is in your own hands. Success is to your credit and failure is your fault. What a heavy and unnecessary burden! The Bible proclaims loud and clear that we are invited to let God be in charge of everything. Do the work put before you, but rest as well. Trust him for the harvest.

HUMILITY

Behind the facade of self-sufficiency lurks an unspoken but powerful assumption: we are capable of taking care of ourselves and therefore don't truly need God at all. Seen in this light, refusal to rest is actually a kind of arrogance. To adopt the sabbath as a way of life requires us to admit we are sheep and not our own shepherd.

PERSPECTIVE

Sabbath reminds us of the true purpose of the abundant life Jesus promised: it is not to work to sustain the body but the steady expansion of the kingdom of heaven on earth. Spend time humbly trusting God to provide the basic necessities of life, and you'll be freed to pursue the kind of spiritual fruitfulness we are meant to have in this life.

SERVICE

Many people object to the idea of restful living because they mistakenly think self-care is *selfish*. In fact, the opposite is true. The person who is exhausted and hounded by stress has little time, energy, or emotional capacity for anyone else. If you do too much to carry responsibility for your life (responsibility that isn't yours), you'll be less able to help someone else as well. Rest to be ready to serve.

There is a time to work and a time to rest. Master the balance in this truth and you'll maximize the gift waiting for you in every moment.

FIFTEEN

FACE YOUR FEAR

*What makes you afraid holds you
back. Here's how to break free.*

It was a sunny summer day in my hometown of Creedmoor,
North Carolina. I was nineteen, driving my Ford Explorer down
Highway 15, singing along with a song on the radio and probably
thinking about the morning's pickup basketball game. My mind was
carefree and my heart untroubled.

That all changed in an instant.

Suddenly, out of nowhere, a black vehicle raced up behind me.
Almost immediately I determined it was an unmarked police car.
After trailing me at close range for half a mile, blue-and-red flashing
lights came on, along with a blaring siren.

I pulled onto an off-ramp and came to a stop on the roadside
shoulder. With guns drawn, two officers ordered me to step out of
my car.

A minute later three other police cars pulled up. As I stood beside
my car with my arms raised over my head, the officers approached,
telling me to put my hands behind my back. A second later my wrists
were in handcuffs.

As officers searched my car, without warrant or apparent cause,
two others flanked me, saying nothing.

"Why was I stopped?" I asked innocently. "What's going on? Why am I being detained?"

My questions were answered with stony silence.

"Can you tell me why I was pulled over? What did I do?"

Again, no answers.

Finally one of the officers motioned me toward the unmarked car, and I was jostled into the back seat, still handcuffed. Leaving my car on the off-ramp, I was taken to a police station and confined to a holding cell with eight other people, some drunk or stoned out of their minds.

After several hours I was escorted to a small interrogation room. Someone pulled my Social Security card from my wallet and accused me of stealing my own identity. I was bombarded with questions.

"What do you do for a living?"

"Where did you get this Social Security card?"

"Have you ever used this Social Security number to get a credit card?"

"Have you ever stolen anything?"

"How did you get your car?"

"Do you have any loans?"

The questioning went on for an hour until a fax arrived: a copy of my birth certificate sent by my mother to prove my identity.

At last I was released.

No citation.

No explanation as to why I had been pulled over.

No apology for being detained behind bars for no reason and no crime.

I paid for a taxi to take me back to the highway off-ramp where my vehicle was parked.

When I got home, I talked through the terrifying experience with my mom. She reminded me of "the talk" she and my father had given me years earlier. They explained I very well could be stopped or detained by law enforcement without provocation, explanation, or justification. It could happen for no other reason than the color of my skin. Their warnings had proven true.

I have experienced many moments of fear in my life, but this encounter with injustice and false accusation ranks high on my list. I was afraid of the unknown and the feeling of helplessness.

Fear is common to all of us. It is universal and universally disliked. In fact, if I were given the task of using only one word to capture the root cause of our troubles as humans, I might choose *fear*. Every corrosive emotion starts there.

- Shame is the fear of judgment.
- Hatred is the fear of others.
- Greed is the fear of lack.
- Jealousy is the fear of not being good enough.

Fill in the blank with any harmful human condition, and I'll argue that fear is part of the soil that feeds it.

No doubt there are moments when acute fear is exactly the right response. The well-known fight-or-flight instinct that kicks in when we are threatened is there to save us from all kinds of danger. If I'm attacked by man or beast, fear is my welcome ally. We can thank God for giving us the healthy, helpful instinct for self-preservation.

But the fear I'm talking about here is something altogether different. The fear that stalks us most often these days is a vague and faceless dread of things we can't even see, much less fight or flee from.

No one is immune to this new kind of angst. We're all afraid of something, and we all pay a price for letting it steer the ship of our lives.

Here are some common examples of things we fear:

- Death (ours or that of someone we love)
- Failure
- Financial insecurity

- Embarrassment
- Loss of respect or esteem
- A host of things that might physically harm us: insects, heights, natural disasters, etc.

For some, runaway fear cripples the mind with severe anxiety. These people often retreat into isolation and defensiveness and require extra help to get out again. In the process, their world and their potential shrinks just as surely as that of a prisoner locked in a cell.

For most of us, however, fear hovers like a layer of fog that never quite lifts. It prevents us from clearly seeing the horizon or enjoying the warmth of a magnificent, sunny life. It undermines our intention to make the very most of *this* day. Here are just a few ways fear impedes our purpose and potential.

FEAR ROBS YOU OF TIME

Paralyzed. That's the word we most often use to describe what it feels like when we're in the grip of fear, unable to move one way or another. In that state, the clock keeps right on ticking. Every passing minute is ripe with opportunities to break the spell and get on with life by facing whatever it is that frightens you (more on that in a minute).

FEAR ROBS YOU OF YOUR HEALTH

Adrenaline is awesome—up to a point. It's meant to arm us with a burst of speed or strength or heighten our senses in a moment of danger. But if we remain in a state of alert all the time, that benefit turns to harm in a hurry. A steady stream of stress hormones can cause everything from headaches and dizziness to heart problems and digestive ailments.[1]

FEAR ROBS YOU OF HOPE

Whatever we dread, it is only one possibility among many. Unchecked fear can cause us to forget that fact and to believe that the unwanted outcome is *inevitable*. Facing our fear can restore our hope in a more abundant future.

BRAVERY ONE MOMENT AT A TIME

Before we unpack some practical tips for how to face our fear and reclaim our right to a magnificent life, let's get something straight about courage. If we don't, the battle with fear may not go as planned. Write this down and post it where you will see it every day, such as your bathroom mirror, refrigerator door, or in your car:

Courage is not a *feeling*.
It is a deliberate choice. It's a decision. It's an action.

People are not either courageous or cowardly, as if bravery were something we either possess at birth or don't, like dark hair or athletic grace. There are simply those who face their fears and those who don't.

The *Oxford English Dictionary* defines courage as "the ability to do something that frightens one."[2] An *ability*, not a superpower, possessed only by the blessed few. In other achievements, we understand that ability is the reward for years of hard work and determination, such as the ability to drive a race car, compose a song, prepare a gourmet meal, or write a novel.

The "ability to do something that frightens one," no matter how it feels at the moment, is no different. The difference between courageous action and paralyzing fear can be generally summed up in a single word: *training*. That is, the work you've done facing small fears, far away from the actual battle and long before the bombardment begins. It's facing fear every day under controlled conditions, convincing your mind it is possible to feel afraid and still do what's best and right in the moment.

But you can only train in the present moment. Today.

Recently I came across a powerful example of someone who overcame fear and hopelessness while in a highly disheartening setting: prison. Young Cyntoia Brown, exploited in her midteens by a sex trafficker, had shot and killed a man who had picked her up. She received a life sentence, and Tennessee law required a minimum of fifty-one years behind bars before parole would be considered. The sixteen-year-old African American wouldn't have a parole hearing until age sixty-seven.

Cyntoia's life was virtually over. Or so it seemed.

Like hundreds of young inmates in similar circumstances, she could have let herself be devoured by the system. Could have let the inevitable prison fear consume her. Maybe join a gang for survival. Become bitter and hardened. Pass the hours, days, and years sleeping and watching TV. Anything to avoid confrontation or harm.

But young as she was and facing at least five decades of confinement, Cyntoia made a choice. Despite the hopeless situation, she would train herself away from fear. She would displace fear with courage.

Through an in-prison educational program, she earned an associate's degree in 2015. She became a mentor for other inmates, encouraging them to pursue high school and college classes. She spearheaded educational opportunities for fellow inmates whose knowledge of English was limited. She earned a bachelor's degree in the spring of 2019.

Her teachers took notice. Social media spread word of Cyntoia's remarkable journey as she helped herself and others to reshape their lives. She radiated hope and purpose. Legal experts as well as celebrities took up her cause.

In early 2019, citing "the extraordinary steps Ms. Brown has taken to rebuild her life," Governor Bill Haslam commuted her sentence, and by August she was released. While she must report regularly to a parole officer, perform community service, hold a job, and participate in counseling, Cyntoia, who's thirty-two years old as I write this, is now free and living a positive, productive life. She's found love and is engaged to a Christian musician.

One of her college teachers said, "[I'm so] thankful and grateful that this young, brave, passionate woman would take this pain and use it for the good of others. . . . I'm so confident in her, absolutely confident."

Cyntoia Brown chose courage. She chose to train in the present moment, even during a hope-smothering prison sentence. She totally turned her life around.[3]

If she could choose courage under near-hopeless circumstances, you can certainly choose courage in *your* present moment. Today, wherever you may be.

More good news? You have 1440 chances to get on with it every single day of your life.

A CAMPAIGN OF COURAGE

All of that looks pretty good on paper, right? But how does it work when the bombs are falling and all your mind wants to do is hide at the bottom of a foxhole? Here's the plan.

DECIDE TO BE FREE

Until you are truly fed up with being pushed around and robbed by your fear, facing it will seem too risky and too hard. Every person on earth is capable of greatness in every moment of every day, but only when the cost of staying stuck seems greater than the risk of stepping out with boldness.

Hockey legend Wayne Gretzky said, "You miss 100 percent of the shots you don't take."[4] What's true on the ice is true in life: you'll never conquer your fear until you make up your mind to give it a shot.

BE CALM AND BREATHE

To face your fear, you have to force it into the open, away from the infinite number of hiding places it can run to. That means bringing it into the only realm where things ever really happen: *the present*. You do that by focusing your mind there and refusing to be drawn into the hall of mirrors of past and future fantasy.

Here's the secret that mystics and sages have known for millennia: your body is always in the present moment. Unlike your thoughts, it can't be anywhere else. So to steer your mind there, focus attention on what your body is experiencing right now. The place to start is with your breath, as is the way mindfulness practices typically do.

Sit comfortably in a chair. Close your eyes and fill your awareness with the sensation of your chest rising and falling as you inhale and exhale. Don't force yourself to breathe a particular way, just let it happen. Feel the cool air moving in and the warm air flowing out. Notice the weight of your body in your chair and the feeling of the floor pushing against your feet. If you're struggling with fear, it will show itself on this open field, where you can deal with it in the present.[5]

Now you're ready for the next step.

NAME YOUR FEAR

Say it out loud. Be specific.

"I'm afraid of being unable to pay the rent next month."

"I'm afraid my relationship with my mother will never heal."

"I'm afraid my boss is looking for a reason to fire me."

Often fears are vague and abstract. We just know we feel afraid and anxious about *something*. It's helpful to pinpoint precisely the source of our fear so we can attack it.

SHRINK IT

Now imagine a close friend has just texted you to confess the very same fear. Visualize picking up your phone and reading it there on the small screen. Even in all caps, it can't be bigger than a few inches! Back in the caverns of your mind, your fear frequently appeared as a giant fire-breathing dragon. By naming and shrinking it, you've made it take a shape and size that will fit into the present.

ANSWER THE TEXT

What would you say to that friend struggling with this fear? Chances are you'd offer them encouragement and comfort. You would remind them they are much bigger than their fear and much more capable of greatness than they realize at the moment. All of this is true—for you as well.

INVENTORY THE PRESENT

Look around. You might be walking through a rough part of town and fear you'll be robbed. You might be afraid you'll get seriously ill. You might fear your boyfriend or girlfriend will end your relationship without warning.

Using all your senses, do you perceive any evidence that what you fear is real and present right now? Nearly always, the answer is no. On those occasions when the answer is yes, you can formulate a proactive, commonsense response. That means you can relax! Looking only at what *is,* you realize that fight or flight is not necessary. Breathe some more and the feeling of peace will begin to deepen.

MAKE A NOW-SIZED PLAN

Pick one thing you can do, right now, to manage the situation you're fearing. The whole dragon can't fit into now. The parts that can fit are the ones you are equipped to handle today.

When I feel anxious about preparing for a weekend seminar,

wondering if I can get everything done in time, it does me no good to look at the entire schedule and agenda of speaking. If I focus, however, on one teaching session at a time, the task is doable. Then I can move on to the next one and the next one. My anxiety turns to anticipation as I shift my perspective to what I can accomplish *now*.

ACCEPT GOD'S INVITATION TO "FEAR NOT"

For people of faith, for those who believe God cares about us and loves us dearly, we know for certain that everything will turn out just fine. It will all be okay. That doesn't mean there won't be pain and worries along the way. But we are sure that God will ultimately make all things right in our lives and in our world.

Here's a promise God made to all of his children: "Do not fear, for I am with you; do not be dismayed, for I am your God. I will strengthen you and help you" (Isa. 41:10). This applies to *you* in every minute of every day.

There is really only one correct way to respond to fear, and that is to face it. We can constructively face our fears by following these three steps.

1. **Discover the foundation of fear.** Fear is often rooted deeply in feelings rather than facts. Pinpoint the emotions connected to the fear to figure out the basis of it.
2. **Acknowledge your fears.** Covering up our fears never fixes them. Something about owning up to our failures helps us deal with the fear of making them.
3. **Focus on what you can do.** For example, I can do my part by controlling my actions, but I can't control the actions of others. I can do my part by planning out my day, but I can't control life circumstances. Remember: it's not what happens to you but how you respond to what happens to you that counts.

NOT A LIFE SENTENCE

During the writing of this book, my wife experienced a major health crisis. For the past seven years, Jen has suffered through several health challenges, and now another came. This time she had extreme pain in her lower left back. It felt severe enough to prompt a trip to the ER.

For me the fear that bubbled up centered on the unknown: what her pain could be and how bad it could become. In the midst of this, I did what most people do when facing a health crisis: I consulted Dr. Google. Do an online search of symptoms and brace yourself for a long list of terrible potential diagnoses and worst-case scenarios. That's exactly what happened as I searched for possible conclusions and outcomes for Jen's symptoms.

It's remarkable how often our minds process and overprocess the likelihood of an unlikely outcome. Fear grips our minds and takes us down the bunny trails of every possible scenario. In our case, each of her tests—blood screening, CT scan, ultrasound, and others—failed to reveal any clear diagnostic information, which compounded my fear. Her doctors decided to move her from one ward to another and to run still more tests.

Adding to the stress, I was not able to be by her side due to the hospital's regulations regarding COVID-19. When she could, between tests, Jen sent me texts. This added to the fear of the unknown, because I could not be there to monitor the situation and help make any of her health decisions.

At the conclusion of the testing, the medical team determined the cause was likely an infection affecting her kidneys. This resulted in numerous days in the hospital for treatment and observation. At last, after an extended time of fretful waiting and wondering, Jen was released from the hospital to recover at home.

What I found to be most fearful in that situation was the unknown of why. The source of our information determines our response to the fear we are experiencing. I did myself no good by gathering data from numerous websites, some credible and some not. My source of information (or misinformation) did nothing to assuage my fears!

Whatever fear you're facing, go first to the ultimate source of strength and courage—your Father God—who will supply all you need to endure hardship and experience freedom from worry.

The prison of fear locks so many of us away from the abundant life we were meant to live, but those bars are an illusion. They look and feel solid, I know. But one courageous step is enough to prove you are as free as you choose to be. Today you have 1440 opportunities to make it so.

SIXTEEN

TODAY, GIVE YOURSELF AWAY

To get into someone else's life, get out of your own.

At 7:00 on a hot August morning in 2014, a woman entered the drive-through of a Starbucks coffee shop in St. Petersburg, Florida. After paying for her iced coffee, she told the employee at the window that she wanted to pay for the order of the driver in line behind her, even though it was a more-expensive caramel macchiato.

Pleasantly surprised, the driver in the car behind paid the kindness forward by paying for the next driver in line as well. And so it went, one driver after another, each passing along an unexpected blessing to the next person in line.

The Starbucks employees started keeping a tally, and by 1:30 p.m., 260 customers had paid it forward. *Eleven hours* after the first woman had started the chain of blessing, a customer finally broke the chain, but not before a total of 378 drive-through customers had happily blessed the customers who followed them.[1]

Up to now our 1440 discussion has focused mostly on ways to enhance our own inner awareness, leave the past behind us, improve our mindfulness, and conquer our fears. All these steps are vital to building a strong life foundation and to making the most of the time God has given us.

There is, however, another essential aspect to fully seizing every minute of every day: looking beyond ourselves and striving to make a difference in the lives of those around us, which will eventually make a difference in the world we live in. Our aim is to *become* better so we can *do* better. To bless others as we have been blessed, even if it's a simple, anonymous blessing like paying it forward at a coffee shop or a fast-food drive-through. We have the power to *bless*.

THE POWER OF BLESSING OTHERS

Have you ever been blessed by someone? I mean truly moved by a person's caring words, selfless actions, or a compassionate embrace just when you needed it? How did it make you feel? Most likely it helped you pause, take a breath, feel calmed and encouraged, and be assured that someone else cares. Maybe it even made you smile.

That's what a blessing does. It takes the initiative to step outside your own life and into someone else's. It takes the time to care and encourage another, to touch someone with empathy and kindness.

Every day, every minute, we have opportunities to make the world a better place by blessing one person at a time.

BLESSING OTHERS IS RECIPROCAL

There's a benevolent irony to giving yourself away, for our Creator designed the act of giving to be reciprocal. When you take time to bless another, you feel good inside, perhaps even better than the recipient. By blessing another, you discover the truth of the timeless proverb,

"The one who blesses others is abundantly blessed; those who help others are helped" (Prov. 11:25 MSG).

When you give of yourself, you also receive blessing. Perhaps immediately, with the wonderful feeling you get inside when you've helped someone. Or perhaps later, in some tangible or intangible way. But the reciprocal blessing definitely happens.

Some unknown sage said, "A person's most useful asset is not a head full of knowledge, but a heart full of love, an ear ready to listen, and a hand ready to help." It's true. The last thing someone wants when in need of encouragement is a treatise of our head knowledge. Rather, they need to see that we love and care, that we're willing to listen and hear, and that we're willing to help if we can.

A PRAYER TO HELP YOU

I can't help thinking of a great hymn our parents and grandparents used to sing, titled "Make Me a Blessing."[2] The chorus ends with the refrain: "Make me a blessing to someone today." I believe the desire expressed by this beloved song should never be out of date, that even now it should be our daily prayer as we seek to bring hope and joy to a world staggering in confusion and darkness.

As you and I work together to make the most of our 1440 daily moments, I encourage you to make this song's refrain your own quick prayer throughout each day: *Make me a blessing to someone today.* Or you might wish to magnify this prayer as part of each morning's spiritual preparation for the day:

God, help me brighten someone's day today.
Show me someone who needs a friend to listen, and give me a heart
*   to truly listen and hear.*
Enable me to encourage someone who needs an affirming word.

Show me where I can offer an authentic act of kindness.
May I take the initiative to lighten someone's load.
Not for my glory, but for yours.

And together let's make a difference.

If you'd like to be the blessing described in this prayer, I welcome you to join with me in making it a daily intention and in living it out. Personally, I can't think of a more meaningful way to invest some of our 1440 precious moments each day.

TAKE THE INITIATIVE

I'm sure you can think of dozens of ways to lighten and brighten someone else's day. The pay-it-forward phenomenon described earlier is a simple and fun way to get started, and there are dozens of variations on that idea. Here are some thoughts for consideration.

- **Show love for those closest to you with a practical act of service.** For family members or others that you live with, do chores that aren't typically your responsibility, offer to run errands for them, bring coffee or breakfast in bed, pitch in to help with a project, or begin the day with a sincere compliment.
- **Write an encouraging note.** It might be simply "Three Things I Appreciate About You," followed by qualities you admire and value about this person.
- **Give a gift card.** Provide a few dollars for a favorite coffee shop or bakery, accompanied with a brief note of appreciation.
- **Send a quick text or email.** "How are you doing?" or "How can I pray for you this week?"
- **Put your phone away when you're with someone.** Maintain eye contact, ask questions, and listen when someone is telling you about his or her life.

- **Do something thoughtful for your coworkers.** Or for the elderly and their caregivers in a nursing home.
- **Encourage a store checkout person.** Smile and tell them they're doing a great job.
- **Write to a teacher or another person who made a difference in your life.** Tell how that individual influenced you and express your appreciation.
- **Compliment someone in front of others.** Genuinely and specifically.
- **Tell a janitor or maintenance person how much you appreciate what he or she does.** "You take good care of us. Thank you."
- **Volunteer your time and talent.** At church, at a charity, or by ringing the bell and spreading good cheer at Christmastime.
- **If you see someone is having a tough day, gently ask,** "How are you doing . . . really?" And be prepared to sit and listen and empathize.
- **Be kind to your servers in restaurants.** Smile and call them by name. Show interest in them as people. Compliment good service. And tip generously—this is how they make their living.
- **Ask a senior citizen about his or her life story.** Truly listen. Ask questions and encourage details.
- **Chat with a homeless person.** Look them in the eye. Ask them to share their story. And don't walk away without offering a cash gift.
- **Serve meals at a homeless shelter.** Thanksgiving, Christmas, Easter, or any time.
- **Compliment a parent** whose kids are behaving. Or encourage someone who is dealing with a misbehaving kid.
- **Pay for someone else's meal in a restaurant.** Perhaps a young family or elderly couple has caught your eye.
- **Let someone in front of you in a grocery line.** Someone behind

you might have only a couple of items or is juggling multiple squirming children.

- **Shovel a neighbor's driveway when it snows or take care of their lawn.** Do not accept or even entertain the notion of payment. You just want to be of help.
- **Bring new coloring books and crayons to children in the hospital.** Or take teddy bears and other encouraging gifts. Double the blessing by taking your own children, or a small group of children from church, to share in the giving.

As you offer the daily prayer and keep your eyes open for possibilities, you will find dozens of other opportunities to reach out and touch others in both big and small ways.

You and I can make a better world one person at a time. Together, let's take a few of those 1440 minutes allotted to us and be a blessing to someone today.

SEVENTEEN

DESTINY IN A DAY

How you live mundane moments reveals how you approach your big-picture purpose.

When I was growing up, I heard something that has stuck with me through the years. I haven't always lived up to its ideal, but when I think of these words, it feels like finding an encryption key that can decode the jumbled cipher of how to live well in a frenzied world.

How you do *anything* is how you'll do *everything*.

I first heard these words from a seasoned basketball coach who was trying to turn a bunch of teenagers into decent people first and then into good athletes capable of playing together as a team. He saw these goals as two sides of the same coin. Even when it came to specific skills of the game, Coach believed a player could be only as good as his or her mastery of the most basic fundamentals.

You can imagine, my teammates and I were more interested in learning to nail the three-pointer or finish a fast break with a crazy dunk than in anything resembling basic skills like footwork or ball handling. You know, the fundamentals. Running sprints for endurance? Forget about it! Get to the part where the arena erupts with applause.

The first time I ever heard Coach utter his memorable advice, he wasn't talking about basketball, at least not directly. He intended to teach us how to *walk*.

That's dumb, I thought.

But he was adamant. At the beginning of practice one day, Coach had us all go back into the locker room and walk onto the floor again. We did, self-consciously, as only teenagers can manage, and gathered around him again.

"Again," he barked. "I said 'walk.' I'm not sure what to call what you just did."

Once more we piled through the doors and out.

"Slouching," he said. "That's the word I'm looking for to describe what I'm seeing. Drifting. Hanging your heads and dragging your feet. You look like a bunch of drifters."

We grumbled, thinking things were getting a little personal now.

Coach threw up his hands and asked his assistant coaches to demonstrate to the drifters how to properly walk onto a basketball court. They went through the locker room doors and immediately reentered. Even we had to acknowledge the difference. The men covered the distance in half the time it took us, backs straight, heads up, eyes forward, arms swinging forcefully at their sides. They walked with purpose and confidence, and when they reached the coach's side, you could tell they were ready for whatever came next.

"Boys, I guarantee, if you walk onto this court like that every day and mean it, that's how you'll practice," Coach said. "If you practice that way, it's how you'll play on game day. And *that's* how you'll win."

But win or lose, he told us, if we mastered our actions in every moment—on and off the court—we couldn't help but be a great team, because we would all be great people. Opponents would remember us. Fans would remember us. We'd succeed at anything we chose to do and never hang our heads again.

GOOD IS THE FOUNDATION OF GREAT

"How you do *anything* [no matter how small] is how you'll do *everything* [no matter how big]."

Sounds simple when you say it like that. But seeing the world this way doesn't come naturally to most people. We like to carve up the contents of our lives—goals, responsibilities, events, relationships—and sort them into two baskets: the extraordinary and the mundane. We treat some things as if they are above (important, meaningful, larger than life) and others as below (trivial, insignificant, boring), and then invest commensurate amounts of energy, time, focus, and commitment in them. We feed the things we find worthwhile and starve everything else. The result is that mediocrity becomes the lowest common denominator in all of it.

The truth is, most of what happens in the precious minutes you are given every day is easy to mistakenly place in the mundane box—doing the laundry, ferrying kids to school, casual interactions with people. To seize the abundant life means living by this indispensable fact: *everything* matters.

TRAITS OF ORDINARY GREATNESS

How do we put this idea into practice? How do we walk onto the court of each day the right way? To succeed, apply the following qualities to everything you do.

INTEGRITY

One dictionary defines integrity as "the quality of being honest and having strong moral principles."[1] Here's how to translate that into living well.

- Step 1: Know what you believe.
- Step 2: Commit to living by those beliefs.
- Step 3: Face up to it when you fall short of the first two.
- Step 4: Do all the above all the time.

It's easy to assume the concept of morality only applies to big-ticket things such as sex, drugs, criminality, etc. Think again. The second entry in that definition of *integrity* is, "the state of being whole and undivided." In other words, living with moral principles means acting as if there is no such thing as big or small in life. There is only *one* thing, namely, your magnificent life.

PRIDE

You know, of course, there are two distinct meanings for this word. There are people who are *prideful*, meaning arrogant, haughty, and smug. And there are those who *take pride* in their work and effort. They demonstrate self-respect, dignity, and honor in what they do and who they are.

I have great admiration for people who take pride in everything they do. They humbly apply themselves with dedication and determination to eventually enjoy a job well done. But some people go through their day the way that my basketball team walked onto the court—slouching. Just good enough appears to be the standard they aspire to in everything, and so it's not surprising that's all they ever achieve.

By contrast, someone who lives with healthy, positive pride displays a fierce determination to complete every action to the highest possible standard, whether or not anyone is watching. To them, maintaining high standards is not negotiable. As a result, opportunity and abundance find *them*.

Martin Luther King Jr. put it like this: "If a man is called to be a street sweeper, he should sweep streets even as Michelangelo painted, or Beethoven composed music, or Shakespeare wrote poetry. He should sweep streets so well that all the hosts of heaven and earth will pause to say, 'Here lived a great street sweeper who did his job well.'"[2]

COURAGE

It's not easy living your beliefs for everyone to see. Commitment to excellence often makes you unpopular, because drifters tend to look bad next to you. It takes bravery to be the one in the crowd who is honest enough and principled enough to swim against the current of good enough.

Decide in every moment that the cost of greatness is a price you are not just willing to pay but *eager* to invest in so as to have a better life.

DISCIPLINE

I once met the matriarch of an old ranching family out west. Her grandson had raised the 4-H grand champion steer at the county fair five years in a row, beating out dozens of other entrants by a wide margin every time. I asked her the secret of her grandson's remarkable success.

"We teach our kids that blue ribbons aren't won at the fair," she said. "They're won when there's a blizzard outside and it's midnight after a long hard day, but the animals still need caring for. Blue ribbons go to those who make a habit of showing up no matter what."

Greatness is, above all, a *habit of discipline*. It is formed in all the difficult moments when we don't feel like doing our best.

COMPASSION

Do you genuinely care how your actions affect others? That can be a powerful motive for doing everything with excellence and integrity. You know that people depend on you to pull your own weight. If you are sloppy in your work—at home or professionally—someone else must take up the slack. Living with compassion means that *matters* to you. Your excellence makes things better for others.

GENEROSITY

People who are truly great in the ordinary moments take compassion to the next level and make it their mission to improve the lives of those around them. They don't just do what they *should* do, they add a layer of generosity. And generosity is often hard, especially when we love the object of our gift more than the recipient of the gift we're giving.

Active generosity makes the world a better place, moment by incremental moment.

In the process you'll find the blessing and abundance you're seeking as well. As Jesus said, "Give, and it will be given to you. Good measure, pressed down, shaken together, running over, will be put into your lap. For with the measure you use it will be measured back to you" (Luke 6:38 ESV).

I am so thankful for my old basketball coach and many others in my life who taught me that pursuing excellence in the small things will lead to excellence in the big things. Sweat and hard work in practice leads to greatness on game day. Dedication when no one is watching leads to success when the spotlight is on.

The same principle applies to every aspect of life: work, relationships, leadership, faith. As we strive to live with integrity and excellence in all ways, we reap the rewards when it matters most. If we aspire to greatness in anything, we should reach for it in everything!

EIGHTEEN

TRANSFORMED THROUGH TRANSPARENCY

*To live fully today—and to make a difference—
let your true self shine through.*

Today you have 1440 chances to do something no one else on the planet will ever have the chance to do.

It's not making money, because many people will get that opportunity.

It's not meeting a new friend, pursuing a dream, learning from a mistake, or falling in love. These are all pretty universal experiences.

King Solomon once lamented there's nothing new under the sun, but there's one experience that is unique to you and new every minute of every day.

That is the opportunity to be you.

That opportunity is yours and yours alone.

I wish early on in my leadership years I had understood this truth. But I didn't. I allowed people's perceptions of me to shape how I led. People's expectations and anticipations, verbalized to me, determined my decisions and methods. I had gone beyond being influenced by people to following, play-by-play, the instructions certain leaders had in mind for my life.

Some people believed I could not effectively lead a church if I didn't wear a suit every Sunday. For a season I wore a suit every Sunday. Others believed I could not effectively lead a church if I had facial hair. So I constantly shaved. Then it dawned on me that I was not living the life God intended for me to live; I was trying to live the life other people wanted me to live. I was tired of being tolerated, so I could fit someone else's identity through me and finally came to the understanding that I cannot live my life to please people.

Living your life to gain the approval of other people diminishes the value and possibility of the life you're called to live.

WHAT ARE YOU HIDING?

We all have aspects of ourselves we're afraid won't be received well by others. Perhaps it's the secret of a past trauma, a recent failure, or a quirky aspect of our personality. Maybe we're convinced we laugh too loudly, which is why whenever we're in groups of friends (especially funny friends) we have to work hard at not dissolving into a fit of raucous snorting.

Or maybe we hide behind the masks and identities we've constructed for ourselves. That creates the feeling the world sees us as responsible, competent adults while we feel like awkward thirteen-year-olds faking our way through grown-up life. (And if you struggle with this feeling, take heart. An estimated seven out of ten of us feel this way at times. So you're in good company.[1])

And, of course, social media doesn't help, does it? We spend hours a day in a virtual reality where people post glimpses of their lives designed to look authentic but which are in fact carefully curated snapshots of their best selves.

The point is it's all too easy to live constantly aware of how we want to appear to people around us, making adjustments in what we say and do to nurture that perception.

Then we wonder why there is a disconnect between who we think we need to be and who we think we really are.

The truth is, men and women have been living in hiding pretty much since the fall of Adam and Eve in the garden of Eden. We may not be cowering behind fig leaves, but we sure spend a lot of time hiding behind facades, masks, pretenses, and images we construct while wearing our finest clothes.

We can tell ourselves all day long that hiding our true thoughts, feelings, desires, values, gifts, shortcomings, and beliefs is fine. That everyone does it. That it isn't hurting anyone.

But it's far from harmless.

Truth be told, it's exhausting.

WHEN WE LIVE INAUTHENTICALLY, BAD THINGS HAPPEN

We know why we hide. We think, If they see the real me . . .

I'll be rejected.

They won't like me.

I won't get what I need.

I'll lose respect or power or influence.

I'll be embarrassed.

No one will understand.

I'll be laughed at.

I'll be alone.

We all understand the why. What we forget, however, is the "but then."

If we were to complete one of the sentences above with full

disclosure, it might read something like this: I'll hide the real me so I won't be rejected, *but then* I'll feel anxious that someone will figure out I'm not who I seem to be.

It's a consequence of hiding our true selves.

The truth is that living authentically ushers a lot of negatives into our lives. Anxiety is one of those, but there are others.

Refusing to let our true selves shine wears us out emotionally, leads to trust issues in relationships, keeps us from addressing the real issues we're avoiding, and lowers our self-esteem.

It also makes us feel isolated. And we *are* isolated. We're isolated because we're virtually unknown. And we're unknown because we're more focused on taking cover than making connections.

And it's stressful.

The stress doesn't necessarily come when we are working hard at managing how we are coming across to others, but from how often our brains wander into the idea that we've got something to hide. Even when we're alone, and there's no one around to perform for, our brains keep wrestling with that gap.

To live fully today and to make a difference today, we have to be fully present and confident. We don't want to be distracted by a brain that keeps returning to the scene of the crime. We don't want to feel fatigued by the effort. We *must* learn to live with authenticity and transparency.

We simply don't have an option.

TO LIVE MORE AUTHENTICALLY, STEP OFF THE STAGE

How do we embrace authenticity?

Let's start with something small: take a break from social media.

Before you can live with genuine transparency and let your true self shine, you have to know and accept yourself. That's hard for any of us to do when we are connected 24/7 with a virtual world characterized by faux transparency.

Even when we think we're being transparent on social media, are we really? (Have you ever posted something authentic and vulnerable while feeling strangely aware of how authentic and vulnerable that post will make you appear to your friends?)

The truth is that it's hard to stop performing for others until we're comfortable stepping off the stage and away from the audience. Once we've got that down and know who we *really* are when no one's watching, we'll be more grounded and prepared to let *that* person shine through even when the onlookers file back into the theater.

TO LIVE MORE AUTHENTICALLY, ACCEPT LOVE JUST THE WAY YOU ARE

It's no wonder we feel the need to perform. If we've bought into the lie that we have to hide our true selves in order to be loved and accepted, it seems like a necessity.

The more we surround ourselves with people who love and accept us with all our quirks, flaws, and foibles, the easier it is to live with authenticity and transparency.

But here's the obstacle: not everyone we meet is able and willing to do that. Heck, we even struggle to accept and love ourselves, don't we? And we're not being completely paranoid when we think that some people, if we let our true selves shine, will reject us. Many won't, maybe most won't, but some people will.

Still, there is someone who loves and accepts us exactly the way we are. And what we experience in our relationship with that someone affects everything. It can empower us to stop performing for others, stop being distracted by our fears of rejection, and start embracing the gift of living well every minute of every day. You know who I mean by someone: God in heaven, he who created you and loves you.

TO LIVE MORE AUTHENTICALLY, FORGIVE AND BE FORGIVEN

Finally, authentic living means owning up to the fact that we're not perfect. Mistakes will be made. If there's any guarantee we get in life, it's that.

Don't use transparency as an excuse to be a jerk. That's never okay. But when things go awry and mistakes are made, forgive yourself. Ask for forgiveness. And grant forgiveness to others too. I emphasize forgiveness continually in my own life and in my messages to others because it is an essential element for joyful living, emotional wellness, and genuine relationships.

When we buy into the lie that mistakes aren't allowed or forgivable, we *have* to hide. We don't have a choice. Because mistakes aren't only inevitable, they are a necessary part of growing and living.

Dr. Phil McGraw describes inauthentic living as you being your "fictional self."[2]

Living well means living real.

Making the most of every minute depends on it.

NINETEEN

DEFEAT YOUR DOUBTS

When doubts surface today, rely
on the true source of faith.

When daylight saving time begins in March, you feel robbed of an hour of much-needed sleep. Even an extra shot of espresso doesn't compensate for the morning grogginess that comes the day after you adjust your clock. When it ends in November, you may temporarily enjoy that extra hour of sleep that night. But it still messes with your inner rhythms. And either way, twice every year, you have to change all your clocks and watches, and if you're like me, you have to pull out some owner's manuals to reset some of them.

Love it or hate it, daylight saving time (DST) is likely here to stay. Contrary to rumor, it wasn't the brainchild of Benjamin Franklin and it wasn't enacted to benefit farmers. (In fact, farmers generally dislike DST because their schedules are determined by sunlight, and when everyone else changes their clocks, it messes with their workdays.) Rather, DST was adopted during the world wars of the last century to conserve energy by capturing more late-day sunlight and reducing the need for evening electricity. It was abandoned after World War II as doubters claimed it was no longer needed. Changing watches and clocks then was almost as big a hassle as it is today.

As if DST wasn't confusing enough, some parts of the United States continued to observe DST while other regions ceased using it. So two decades after World War II, Congress passed the Uniform Time Act, calling for DST to begin every April and end every October. In 2005 the Energy Policy Act stretched DST from March to November. But Congress did not require all states and territories to comply. Most do but a few still do not.

A GOOD CONFUSION?

Yet despite its drawbacks, detesters, and doubters, there is a case to be made that daylight saving time is actually a good thing. While it may mess with our brains and bodies for a day or two each spring, it also offers a more natural, sunnier life overall. A March 2020 *Popular Mechanics* article contended, "In reality, DST is an eight-month experiment designed to make life, well, more pleasurable for humans. In the Western world, we typically spend more awake time in the evenings than in the mornings. We also enjoy many benefits from being awake in the sunshine. [We enjoy] vitamin D, increased exercise, increased socializing, and overall improvements to mental health that come with sunlight."

Additional daylight at the end of the day gives us extra time to do yardwork, play outside with our kids, engage in outdoor sports, or enjoy an evening walk. "Absent DST," the article concluded, "for eight months per year, our days would not be structured to enjoy the most sunlight possible."[1] There is also substantial evidence that, in addition to conserving energy, the extra hour of sunlight helps reduce crime during the daylight hours.

DST might actually be good for us after all. A couple of groggy days in March is worth the exchange for months of energy savings, improved health, and natural evening light to illumine recreation and further productivity.

This small, temporary idea that has become part of our lives and totally changed how we view time today has benefits that outweigh its drawbacks. And like many beneficial ideas, DST has also had its vocal critics and doubters all along.

As do many useful ideas.

In fact, you may be hearing voices of doubt and criticism about an idea or dream of your own.

THE DEVIOUS WHISPER

They come out of the blue. From left field. And even from the pit of hell. There you are, minding your own business, investing a few of your 1440 minutes to become the person God designed you to be, when suddenly you hear them. They begin as a mere whisper.

You can't do this. You're not good enough.

Not smart enough. Not good-looking enough.

Then they grow a little louder.

She's so much better at this than you are.

It's gonna be an epic fail, like always.

And louder . . .

Is God really there? Does he really care?

How can he love you when your life's going this way?

Voices. You hear them. I hear them. They may start as devious whispers, but if we give them more than a moment's attention, they can quickly rise to a carping disruption in our soul. They may cause us to hesitate or to make a rash decision or to abandon our quest altogether.

They are voices of doubt.

THE DREAM DASHERS

Ever since the sneaky serpent lied to Eve in the garden of Eden, the Devil has been whispering lies to God's people. He told Eve that God surely was fibbing about the Tree of Knowledge of Good and Evil. She ate the fruit, and then Adam ate the fruit, and in doing so they set in motion millennia of battles between good and evil—battles that still rage. (I know who wins in the end. I've read the book. But just a reminder that it's still going to be rough between now and then.)

Adam and Eve heeded the voice of doubt. And their dream of living forever in the paradise called Eden was dashed for good.

Through the eons since, the same Enemy has been devoted to lying about God and to hurting God's children. We know at some point this slimy serpent gets his comeuppance in the end, but until that glorious day, it seems like he's doing everything he can to sabotage and weaken God's kingdom, even down to the doubts and dream dashers that creep into our thoughts.

THE MASTER LIAR

The Bible tells us that Satan has been granted temporary status as "the prince of the power of the air" (Eph. 2:2 ESV), meaning that he is able to wreak deceit, failure, illness, tragedy, and chaos on earth, even among God's people. He is a master counterfeiter and liar, working tirelessly to get us to worship him instead of God.

He's also working tirelessly to deceive you and me by whispering lies to discourage our dreams, to weaken our resolve to trust and follow God and do his will with our lives.

He is the dream destroyer, the voice of doubt.

He is our adversary. Our enemy. He is committed to deceiving and disheartening us and weakening God's kingdom. We must be aware of his tactics so we can stand strong against his assault. Fortunately, we have been equipped to fend off doubts and deceptions: "For God has not given us a spirit of fear, but of power and of love and of a sound mind" (2 Tim. 1:7 NKJV).

In other words, we're locked and loaded.

So when doubts creep into our thinking—and they will—we can stand strong. We can respond with the power and sound mind the Creator has given us.

WHO ARE YOU LISTENING TO?

When it comes to sorting through the whispers and potential dream killers, a friend of mine has learned to ask himself, "Who am I listening to?" He's found that if the whispers and questions belittle him as a person or minimize the truth of God's Word, then they most likely are not from God but from the Enemy. Samples of these malevolent whispers and words are:

> *Who are you to try to accomplish this?*
> *You'll never measure up.*
> *You moron, why did you do that?*
> *You're not strong enough.*
> *You failed before. You're gonna fail again.*
> *If you're getting resistance, God can't be behind this.*
> *God doesn't love you if you're going through this.*
> *Satan is a myth.*
> *What if the whole God-and-heaven thing isn't true?*

When you hear whispers of doubt and dream dashing, words of self-derision, or anything that casts shade on the goodness and truth of God, ask yourself that all-important question:

Who am I listening to?

Between God and our spiritual enemy, who talks this way?

Who wants you to be discouraged?

Who wants you to hate yourself?

Who wants you to fail and embarrass God's kingdom? To doubt God and his Word?

You know the answers. It's the deceiver himself, Satan. Don't fall for the lie that he doesn't exist. God's Word warns us that he's alive and highly active. He knows he's already lost the war, but he's a sore loser. He's causing as much havoc as he can before God takes him down for good. He wants to bring *you* down, and he doesn't care how hard. The Enemy can be one of the most patient and persistent voices you hear if you allow his voice to take root in your mind.

Don't listen to him. Cast down every thought, every negative voice, and every skewed perspective he presents. Identify lies that are creeping into your mind, and replace them with the truth found in Scripture. When you hear a voice in your head saying you're worthless, inferior, and defective, make a choice to listen to the voice of God, who says you are valuable, cherished, and indispensable.

WHEN GOD WHISPERS

Thank God that he holds you in his almighty hand. Ask him for his clear guidance. "Be still," he says, "and know that I am God" (Ps. 46:10).

He is God. He is our true source of faith and strength.

Our. Only. True. Source.

He speaks truth, guidance, affirmation, love. Yes, he'll point to areas you need to work on and shortcomings that need improvement, for he is holy and wants you to be holy. But he will never demean or belittle you. He will never cast doubt on himself or on his Word. Invite him to be part of your daily life, and he will accompany you, closely, on your journey.

Back when one of God's people was about to embark on a big-time dream, God whispered to him, "Be strong and courageous. Do not be afraid; do not be discouraged, for the LORD your God will be with you wherever you go" (Josh. 1:9).

Those are the kinds of words God says. And aren't they *so* worth listening to?

TWENTY

THE POWER OF PERSPECTIVE

Your reality is determined by how you view it.

Years ago I learned a simple yet profound lesson at the dining room table of my mentor. As we sat across from each other, he pushed a basket of fruit between us.

"What do you see?" he asked.

I immediately responded, "Well, I see an apple."

"Is that all?" he said. "Tell me what else you see."

I replied, "Okay, I also see a bunch of grapes, oranges, and bananas."

He nodded and said, "Good. And now let me tell you what I see. I'm looking at strawberries, peaches, plums, and apricots. All right there in front of me."

I waited, knowing there was a lesson to be learned from this exercise, as there had been many times before with similar exercises.

Finally, he said, "We're both looking at the same basket of fruit, right? It's sitting there between us. It looks inviting and delicious. But we're describing different things. We're naming different kinds of fruits depending on where we're sitting and what we're seeing from our individual point of view.

My mentor was absolutely right. Oftentimes we could be looking at the same thing, but based on where we stand or the season of life we're in, our experience shapes our perspective. And our perspective on all kinds of things—problems, faith, relationships, career—largely determines our actions and attitudes.

PERCEPTION VERSUS REALITY

Since the days of Isaac Newton, Francis Bacon, and René Descartes, society has embraced the idea that the material world exists "out there." According to this view, the reality we observe with our senses is the way it is, and can only be that way, because of the fixed laws of physics and nature.

We acknowledge that everything in the universe is in motion and constantly shifting through stages of development and decline. Even so, we accept that what we can see, hear, taste, touch, and smell simply *is*, with no room for interpretation. Until recently, this assumption formed the basis of all scientific discovery.

At the beginning of the twentieth century, however, cracks formed in this view of things. Early quantum physicists said, "Not so fast," and proceeded to demonstrate that we are not passive observers of an objective reality, like spectators at a circus. Rather, we are in *relationship* with what is and we constantly influence what shape it takes. That's because, in addition to our senses, another human force is in play: our *thoughts*.

If this blows your mind a little, you are not alone. Even scientists in the thick of this research are amazed by their findings. Niels Bohr, one of the fathers of quantum physics, quipped, "If quantum mechanics hasn't profoundly shocked you, you haven't understood it yet."

Don't worry. You don't have to master advanced math to wrap your head around this stunning principle and put it to good use in your quest for maximum magnificence in every moment of your life. As brainy as it all sounds, this idea has down-to-earth practical benefits for us all. We'll get to some hands-on ways to make this real in your life in a moment. But first, here's a little bit more science to make the case further.

YOUR BRAIN IS A CARETAKER

It turns out that you need far more than a pair of eyes to see or ears to hear. Your physical senses are excellent tools for gathering raw information about your environment. But the action of photons striking your retina alone doesn't constitute what we think of as sight. If the process stopped there, you'd have seen nothing.

These photons hitting your eyes require *interpretation*.[1]

Enter your brain. More important, enter your *mind*.

Your brain takes the data gathered by your senses and processes it into the images you see. It filters, sorts, prioritizes, and, yes, interprets all that data. It correlates the emergent picture with visual memories of other such scenes you have observed in the past. That comes in handy since it means you don't have to relearn what a tree is over and over.

From a purely biological point of view, the brain has three main goals here: *your safety, sustenance,* and *success.*

Like any good caretaker, it looks first for those things that might pose a threat and then for the stuff you may need and want in life. Then it prioritizes any information that will help you accomplish a short-term goal, like winning a pickup game of basketball or planting flowers in your garden. Your brain largely ignores everything else your senses may detect in the moment.

So far, that description accounts only for the nuts-and-bolts perceptions your brain uses to do its job. That is, it's sorting out the material factors that shape your immediate view of the world: the speed and distance of oncoming traffic, whether the milk in the refrigerator has gone bad, the attractive person in the coffee shop you might like to get to know better.

But there is another set of filters at work in the process, and it's arguably even influential in shaping your experience of life.

THE POWER OF BELIEF

Here's where it gets really interesting for those of us setting out to create our best possible life. Coupled with what your senses *seem* to say is true, your view of reality is also shaped by what your mind *believes* to be true for reasons of its own.[2]

Suppose you are in a situation that requires you to walk alone through an inner-city alley late at night. You don't directly see or hear any evidence that someone waits in a darkened doorway to attack you. But you are conditioned to believe that dark alleyways are *always* dangerous. Suddenly your body is flooded with adrenaline. Your heart rate quickens and your breathing grows shallow. Your palms sweat as you pick up your pace. Now your senses start to play tricks on you, seeming to see and hear things that aren't really there. What your mind believes in advance to be real causes your body to react in the moment exactly the same way as if the threat were *actually* real.

Everyone has experienced some version of this scenario in which some deeply held belief took priority over actual sensory evidence and created the conditions you hoped to avoid.

This effect can snowball as we live our lives, creating conditions we didn't realize we had any control over. Each of us forms beliefs throughout our lives based on what we've been taught by parents, teachers, spiritual leaders, and peers; what we've personally experienced in the past; and things we pick up from news reports or other media sources. Our beliefs are even influenced by inherited fears and prejudices that seem to have no rational basis. Sometimes, as in the dark alley example, the effect is clearly detrimental. Learning to recognize your mind at work in this way is a great step toward health and well-being.

But guarding yourself against negative perceptions is only part of the story. The real power lies at the other end of the spectrum, where we are able to take control of the process and consciously steer our thoughts and beliefs where *we* choose. If our experience of reality is shaped by our perception of it and that perception is shaped by our mind, then why would we waste another moment mired in negative and limiting thoughts and beliefs? Knowing God has made you with a powerful brain and the ability to filter your thoughts, why go on pretending you are a helpless victim of the way things are? Why indeed?

PURIFIED PERCEPTION

Here are four steps you can take today to shape your own reality.

1. **Think for yourself.** Question things you've been taught or heard that raise doubts in your mind. Challenge the assumptions you've formed through past experiences.
2. **Improve your mental diet.** Take a break from nonstop news channels. Step away from social media. Abstain from entertainment sources that leave you feeling fearful, depleted, or degraded.
3. **Take charge of your self-talk.** Notice what your mind is saying about you, and replace negative messages with confidence-building affirmations. Instead of telling yourself, "I've blown it in the past and will again this time," tell yourself, "I've learned from past mistakes and will do much better this time." Instead of telling yourself, "I'm just not as talented as other people," tell yourself, "I have my own unique talents that I can use to the fullest." If your unfounded beliefs about dark alleys can create a fearful reality, then think what positive thoughts can do!

4. **Visualize the reality you want to create and ask God for it!**
   Jesus said, "Until now you have asked for nothing in My name;
   ask and you will receive, so that your joy may be made full"
   (John 16:24 NASB).

In this very moment, you have all you need to create the life you desire
and that you were created by God to enjoy. Believe it!

TWENTY-ONE

FOLLOW THE LEADER

An extraordinary act of God begins with
an ordinary act of obedience.

In the next twenty-four hours you have 1440 shots to seize the power of the day and, in the process, transform your life and maybe even the world. If that sounds like a lot of opportunities, it is. But don't just assume that with *that* many golden coins to spend, you'll undoubtedly stumble into spending some of them well, even if some are wasted.

No, to fill your days with delight instead of drudgery, impact instead of impasse, and adventure instead of apathy, it takes intentionality *and* the right role models. Indeed, your 1440 chances to be remarkable will yield less than you might imagine if you are influenced by the wrong leaders.

Don't get me wrong, we're all influenced by the society we live in. Our culture. Our peers. Social media. Other people. There are plenty of people to admire out there, but only one worth truly following.

What leader are you following?

When we choose to be followers of Jesus and his way of life, we know the name of our leader, but how intentional are we at following him into deeper relationship, emulating his actions, and obeying his commandments?

TO MAKE YOUR DAY MATTER, FOLLOW HIM

To make the most of your 1440 minutes, start with following the person of Jesus, not just his actions. Respond to his welcome before trying to replicate his works. Chase intimacy over imitation.

Why? Jesus explained it like this: "Many will say to me on that day, 'Lord, Lord, did we not prophesy in your name and in your name drive out demons and in your name perform many miracles?' Then I will tell them plainly, 'I never knew you. Away from me, you evildoers!'" (Matt. 7:22–23).

I've always been intrigued by this verse. Did these doers think they were being sincere? Did they think they knew Jesus? Did his words surprise them? If I were to hazard a guess, I'd say they weren't as shocked as we might think. After all, you *know* if you know someone or not. You know if you are pursuing intimacy or simply perfecting an impersonation.

Understand the distinction. Intimacy with the person of Jesus Christ is the foundation upon which everything else will rest.

TALK WITH GOD

We should talk and have conversations with God just as we do with other humans. God talks to us through his general Word, the Bible, and through his specific Word, the leading of the Holy Spirit.

MAKE IT PERSONAL

We have to make things with God personal and intimate, so intimate that the relationship transcends words. True intimacy with God is felt deep within your soul. It's there that you bond with the heart of God.

BE PATIENT

Just as developing intimacy with my wife took time, so it is with my relationship with God. As you grow in trust with him and believe more and more what he says in his Word, your love for him will increasingly grow.

TO OPTIMIZE EACH MOMENT,
FOLLOW HIS EXAMPLE

Many times the Bible tells us to model our actions after the actions of Jesus. For instance, the apostle John wrote, "Whoever claims to live in him must live as Jesus did" (1 John 2:6). Jesus himself said as much during his last supper on earth. He washed the feet of each of his disciples, and then he said, "Now that I, your Lord and Teacher, have washed your feet, you also should wash one another's feet. *I have set you an example that you should do as I have done for you.* Very truly I tell you, no servant is greater than his master, nor is a messenger greater than the one who sent him. Now that you know these things, you will be blessed if you do them" (John 13:14–17, emphasis added).

This week read through one of the four New Testament Gospels. Pay attention to how Jesus responded to people around him, how he interacted with his Father, how he handled persecution. Observe how he responded to temptation in the wilderness. Pay attention to how he actively used Scripture. Make note of how he loved on those who were marginalized, how he equipped those who believed in him, and how he ministered. Finally, observe how he was obedient to his Father, even when his obedience resulted in great personal sacrifice.

As the clock ticks away and you receive the gift of another minute, make it remarkable by using it to follow the example set before you by the One you love.

TO LIVE IN LOVE, KEEP HIS COMMANDMENTS

Could Jesus have put it any more clearly than this: "If you love me, keep my commands" (John 14:15)?

If you were raised by a harsh, authoritarian father, you may be tempted to think of God in the same light. It's easy to do. Assign to an invisible God the traits and personality of our very visible parents.

But just because it's understandable and easy to do doesn't make it right.

The truth is that God's commandments are rooted in love. He created them in love, delivered them in love, and uses them to equip us to love and serve others.

So it shouldn't be any surprise that Jesus wants us to be motivated by love as we follow him.

"We know that we have come to know him if we keep his commands. Whoever says, 'I know him,' but does not do what he commands is a liar, and the truth is not in that person. But if anyone obeys his word, love for God is truly made complete in them" (1 John 2:3–5).

Of course, to obey the commandments of Jesus you have to understand what they are. Read about many of Jesus' commandments to us in his own words, and make a regular study of the Bible part of your life.

TO EMBRACE THE EXTRAORDINARY, ACT IN HIS AUTHORITY

Miracles happen when we spend our minutes trying to understand and obey Jesus' commands. God is able to move in our lives and in the lives of those around us in ways that exceed our wildest dreams: "Very truly I tell you, whoever believes in me will do the works I have been doing, and they will do even greater things than these, because I am going to the Father. And I will do whatever you ask in my name, so that the Father may be glorified in the Son. You may ask me for anything in my name, and I will do it" (John 14:12–14).

Spending your minutes doing these things empowers you to live with confidence and conviction, knowing you are a valued child of the King. And when you do, prepare to be amazed at the results.

Seemingly ordinary acts of obedience can usher in extraordinary acts of God.

Have you ever pondered the fact that life can pivot in a single moment? For some reason we're more inclined to remember the days we felt traumatized, when life took a turn for the worse in a single devastating instant.

And yet the opposite happens, too, and if we take a few moments to reflect on it, we'll undoubtedly remember times in our lives when a single moment changed everything for the better. When God intervened in a way that we can't deny and can't explain away.

We're not always privy to what ushered in that moment, but when we're in heaven and all mysteries are revealed, I believe we'll discover that what predicated each miracle was a simple act of obedience. Maybe you were obedient and in time reaped the results of that choice. Maybe someone else was obedient, and you received a miracle as a result.

In the same manner, I believe your every act of obedience ultimately unleashes a miraculous act of God in your life or in the lives of others. Maybe you'll see evidence of it, maybe you won't. But when we spend our golden minutes walking in our God-given strength, life is anything but business as usual.

If you believed, really believed how you spend your 1440 minutes could change the trajectory of lives and events, wouldn't you take these minutes a lot more seriously?

I know it's a huge paradigm shift. After all, we've spent years trudging through our days, passing the time, waiting for those occasional moments when the stars seem to align and we feel truly alive.

What a different perspective to realize that we can live each minute to its fullest and that how we live each moment can move the very hand of God and unlock untold blessings. We all have many leaders we might listen to and learn from: political leaders, corporate leaders, spiritual leaders, thought leaders. All of them might have valuable things to teach us. But when we follow Jesus, our true leader, we will carry with us throughout each day the love, compassion, and boldness he exemplified. That is a leader worth following!

TWENTY-TWO

FIND FREEDOM IN FORGIVENESS

*By forgiving those who hurt you, you free
yourself to be fully alive every day.*

Imagine you are carrying a laundry basket overflowing with dirty gym socks. In fact, you carry it everywhere you go. It's heavy and takes both arms to hold. This basket contains nasty socks dating all the way back to your days in middle school. There are a couple of moldy T-shirts in there too. Plus an old shoe.

A pungent vapor surrounds you, but because you never put the basket down, you've grown used to it. Your friends and family have learned to ignore it too. Once in a while someone gently suggests maybe it's time to do your laundry, but mostly nobody gives it much thought anymore.

One day you meet someone new who takes in the scene with a fresh perspective.

"Wow," they say. "What's up with the toxic socks?"

"What are you talking about?" you ask.

"*That!* The festering pile of fungus you have there. Doesn't it make your eyes water?"

"Oh, this?" you say. "No, this is good. I carry it for a reason."

"Really? Why?"

You answer matter-of-factly, "I've saved these socks from every game when I was fouled by some rotten cheater on the court. They help me to see it coming the next time and to keep it from happening again."

"Hmm," your new friend says, noticing how the socks have piled up over the years. "How's that working out for you?"

A FOUL LOAD

Totally ridiculous, right? Nobody in their right mind would do that. If we're talking about an actual pile of stinking socks, I'd have to agree with you. But by now you've caught on that this scene describes something much less obvious and way more damaging: the habit we all have of carrying around old offenses and wounds until they stink up our current lives.

It is called *unforgiveness*. Few things will rob you of your endowment of opportunity for fulfillment and abundance in every minute quicker than this.

How? Imagine one day, while you're carrying your basket, I offer you a chest of glittering treasure: gold, rubies, emeralds, diamonds, priceless coins. All yours, no strings attached. But there's one thing you have to do first. Surely it's easy to see what that is.

You must put down the basket to receive the treasure.

Unforgiveness occupies the mental and emotional space that could be filled with growth and contentment. You can't hold both at once.

Here are five reasons why.

UNFORGIVENESS TRAPS YOU IN THE PAST

I've shared already in previous chapters that to lay hold of this treasure you must be mindfully *present*. Wounds and offenses you've suffered in the past can only ever exist there—in the past. Hanging on to them, mentally reliving the awful details again and again, rehearsing what you wish you had said or done differently, imagining vengeful retribution—all these chain your mind to a moment that is long gone. The past holds none of the potential we've been seeking to foster or the opportunity we hope to seize. Mental time spent there is barren and empty.

Remember: forgiving the one who harmed you is never about letting them off the proverbial hook. It's about freeing *yourself* and reclaiming your inheritance of abundance in the now.

UNFORGIVENESS DOMINATES YOUR IMAGINATION

Elsewhere in these pages I've shared the mind-blowing truth that you create what you think. Another way to say that is "You are what you think." This bit of wisdom dates back at least to the book of Proverbs (for example, see 23:7). It's true. Thoughts are powerful blueprints that shape your reality whether you are aware of it or not.

This means the first step in creating an awesome life in every moment is to *visualize* all that you want to be, do, and have in vivid detail. To borrow some tech jargon, it takes a lot of mental bandwidth to form and hold that picture in your mind. Reliving a past offense over and over is like malware that launches a denial-of-service attack, pushing every other thought aside.

Let the past go to see your future self grow.

UNFORGIVENESS HINDERS HEALING

You may be tempted to point out an obvious flaw in my reasoning. "The event that caused me harm may be in the past," you say, "but my *pain* is still very real in the here and now. Just letting go doesn't make that go away."

And you are right—to a point.

It's true that forgiveness may not automatically make you feel better. It is a choice, not an emotion.

Forgiveness is the difficult decision to stop picking at your wounds and to let God's healing commence. You can choose to stop ruminating over a past offense. You can choose to stop replaying in your mind the hurtful words said to you. You can choose to address painful experiences rather than let them fester.

Rule number one, if you want to get better, stop making things worse.

UNFORGIVENESS DAMAGES YOUR RELATIONSHIPS

Anyone who has been in a troubled relationship will recognize another word to describe old hurts and grievances we can't seem to put down: *baggage.* It is code for unresolved issues that can make your present partner feel as if they must compensate for offenses they did not commit. It's not only you who has to deal with the fallout, it's them. It's an unfair burden and a real stumbling block to creating healthy relationships based on what is true *now.* Why saddle them permanently with the pain of your past?

Forgiveness is how you drop the baggage and walk away from it for good.

UNFORGIVENESS IS NOT GOD'S WAY

Thank goodness! Where would we be if God kept track of all our failings? To claim a magnificent life in the present, we must align ourselves with all that God wants for us *and* also with all that God *is.* The apostle Paul summed it up like this:

> Let all bitterness and wrath and anger and clamor and slander be put away from you, along with all malice. Be kind to one another, tenderhearted, forgiving one another, as God in Christ forgave you. (Eph. 4:31–32 ESV)

Why do any of this? Because those rotten gym socks you've been carrying around are stinking up your life and your relationships.

It might be that you're avoiding someone who has hurt you, unable to make eye contact with them and with no inclination to make even small talk.

It might be that you secretly dream up ways to get back at a wrongdoer, savoring the opportunity for vengeance.

It might be that you resist opening up or getting close to others, protecting yourself from being harmed again.

These could be signs that unforgiveness is still part of your life, preventing the freedom and wholeness God intends for you. Through his power, you can release what is weighing you down and holding you back.

TWENTY-THREE

MOTIVE MATTERS

Faith isn't just what you do—it's why you do it.

Competitive cyclist Lance Armstrong seemed invincible. Famous and admired for overcoming cancer and winning seven consecutive Tour de France victories, he earned multiple millions each year in endorsements. His success also helped raise nearly $400 million for the Lance Armstrong Foundation (now the Livestrong Foundation) to help and encourage others in their fight against cancer.

But then the rumors started, and Armstrong vehemently denied them. Whispers continued. The swirling accusations caused the foundation to distance itself from Armstrong, and contributions slid significantly. Then, after years of more victories and denials, Armstrong finally confessed to doping, that is, taking illegal performance-enhancing drugs. His claims to winning clean and drug-free had been a con. One commentator said in *Forbes* magazine that when Armstrong chose to break the rules, "He betrayed millions of people who believed in him, and risked the reputations and careers of teammates in order to win personal glory."[1]

In his 2013 confession-interview with Oprah Winfrey, Armstrong was quick with the "everyone else is doing it" defense. His reason and his why was that because everyone else was doping, his doing so was a necessary evil. He had conned officials, competitors, fans, and Livestrong contributors in the belief the bluff was tolerable because other cyclists also participated in under-the-table doping.

Before the charade collapsed in scandal, Armstrong's domination of the sport had brought him and his foundation millions. And it took years of whistleblowing as well as a lengthy investigation by the US Anti-Doping Agency to corner Armstrong into admitting the truth. Victory, dynasty, profit, reputation—his *why*—all had driven him to put self before others, embrace dishonest practices, and keep them under wraps for as long as possible.

Today, his legacy is one of deception and disrepute.

GETTING THE WHY RIGHT

Future sociologists may well look back on our time and call it the age of the ulterior motive. The era of the con, scam, and endless spam. Far too often what looks to be a great deal turns out to be a *raw* one instead. Things that seem too good to be true frequently are just that.

The old saying "Never look a gift horse in the mouth" was coined during a more innocent time. Sadly, it is no longer as wise as it once was. It used to mean, "It's rude to be suspicious when someone tries to do something for you." But these days, when so many gift horses turn out to be of the Trojan variety, packaged to look good on the outside but concealing harm within, skepticism is a matter of prudent self-defense. If we've grown jaded, it's because of necessity.

At first, you might wonder why I'm suddenly bringing you down like this. What good is such a dark assessment in a book about seizing the fantastic potential for abundant living God has placed in every moment? After all, *The Power of 1440* isn't about what's wrong with the world but about all that can be right, *very* right, with your life if you'll take advantage of what's right in front of you here and now.

The purpose of this chapter is to convince you it's not enough to learn a few proven tips and tricks for creating a better life. Bookstore self-help sections are stuffed with this year's version of that kind of plan because last year's program turned out to be as ineffectual at producing real change in people's lives as ever. If that's the kind of secret insight you thought you'd gain by reading this book, this is where I must disappoint you by insisting that reaching your God-given potential is not so much about changing *what* you do as *why* you do it. In fact, if you get the *why* right, the details of *how* and *what* will come much more easily.

Because your motive matters.

WHAT LIES BENEATH

Think again about the conman culture I described above. People who make their living by cheating others don't get up in the morning and rub their hands together in evil glee at how much fun it's going to be to rob an elderly widow of her life's savings. Chances are, they've trained themselves not to think of that consequence at all, to sideline their conscience and fortify their resolve. Misguided as they are, these are people, after all, whose hearts and minds work the same way as ours.

They are able to do what they do because they have an entirely different *motive* that overrides every other consideration. Their *why* is very simple: to make as much money as possible, as fast as they can, by whatever means are available.

"Thank goodness that doesn't describe me!" you might say. Let's hope not! Still, none of us should be quite so hasty in pronouncing our motives to be pure. The truth is, money is not the only motivation that can warp what you do and blind you to its effects. Even when your actions appear sound enough on the surface, what lies beneath them can spoil the end result.

Here are some of the most common misplaced motives.

FEAR

The list of fears that drive us is seemingly endless. We act as we do because we're afraid of failure, rejection, embarrassment, disappointment. We fear boredom, discomfort, hardship, lack, being alone or left out. When fear matters most, it makes us timid and indecisive, qualities that work against opportunity and abundance every time.

APPEARANCES

Sometimes what matters most to us is how our actions look to others and what they may think of us as a result. When this is your *why*, your actions are limited to things that will safely manage perceptions and protect your image, even if they undermine your desire to live your best life in every moment. The truth is, most people think about you far less than you imagine they do, so choices aimed at pleasing them are nearly always wasted.

MANIPULATION

Manipulation is trying to get others to do what you want them to do or to be other than they are, and it can be a powerful reason for behaving the way you do. For instance, if taking steps to lose weight is meant to be a subliminal message to someone else that they should do the same, that's a motive that is unlikely to accomplish either goal. It won't be enough to sustain you through the hard work of true transformation, and few people respond to coercion, no matter how well intended it is.

COMPETITION

What's wrong with being motivated by a desire to win? In sports, nothing at all, so long as victory doesn't come at the cost of fairness.

Nor in business if success can be had without ruining someone else in the process. How much better would it be to let *service* be your reason for playing the game?

HABIT

Often the most deeply ingrained motives are those we aren't aware of. We do things a certain way because that's the way we've *always* done them. Chances are these are inherited ways of thinking. If you've made the decision to take charge of your life and lay hold of every ounce of opportunity available to you, now is a good time to examine your habitual reasons *why*.

ONE GUIDING STAR

A person's reasons for doing what they do can be notoriously tricky to see, much less untangle. That's part of what psychotherapy is all about and why it can often take years of talk to get to the bottom of your behavior.

Thankfully, Jesus simplified the whole subject by giving us one overarching motive to weed out what doesn't fit and to unify everything that does. It's contained in the way he taught us to pray: "Your kingdom come, your will be done, on earth as it is in heaven" (Matt. 6:10).

Why do we lay claim to the magnificent treasure of opportunity in our endowment of minutes each day? To better live as God wants, in alignment with and allegiance to his kingdom.

Embrace *that* and all other motives become easier to see and to avoid.

Think of what kind of world we would live in if we

1. entered every financial transaction with a desire to see everyone blessed,

2. approached every relationship determined to give the other the best we have to offer,

3. made it our most pressing *why* to see that no one goes homeless or hungry ever again, and

4. put love above every other consideration at all times.

A world like that would look much different from the one we inhabit today. We all long for that. And we all have the ability to move our world toward harmony rather than division, peace rather than discord, compassion rather than contention. Each day you and I can use our minutes to show those around us that the kingdom of God is alive and well on Planet Earth.

TWENTY-FOUR

STEP ONE

*Whatever you dream of doing, the
beginning will fit into a day.*

Melanie knew she needed to do something about her weight. Three years ago her doctor told her she was carrying about thirty-five extra pounds for a woman her size, and now those thirty-five pounds were still there, plus an additional six. Three years of broken New Year's resolutions. Three years with no visible progress in her mirror or her bathroom scale.

And there was a good reason Melanie felt stuck in weight-loss and fitness ambitions. She'd never actually followed through on her resolve. Instead, she had told herself, "Someday I'm gonna get this weight off. Someday I've got to get to the gym."

But her *somedays* were always "some other day" and never "today is the day." Today never felt quite right. Today was too busy. Today was too depressing. She just didn't have the energy today, and someday always sounded better. So for Melanie it had been three years of somedays.

Good intentions, bad follow-through. She just couldn't seem to take the first step.

And there's Jeff, a middle-aged man who has always dreamed of writing a novel. For years he's been plotting a spellbinding story in his head. He conjured characters and invented twists and turns. He even drove two states away to scout a small town as a possible setting for the story. It was all starting to come together. A bestseller, Jeff believed, with a possible movie option with a major studio. Get Spielberg or Scorsese on the line!

Except Jeff just couldn't start to write anything down. He'd taken his laptop to the coffee shop several times, because he'd heard that J. K. Rowling had written her first Harry Potter novel in coffee shops. But Jeff found that people watching and web surfing went better with his caramel macchiato, and by the time he finished sipping and surfing, his mental energies had expired. He'd try again tomorrow.

His next attempt was at a quiet table in the local library. But first he thought he'd browse the bookshelves and see what his next read would be. And he browsed and browsed, and an hour later he went home with a book to read but nothing written.

Jeff tried opening his laptop in a spare bedroom at home. But it wasn't long before the phone rang, and then his children needed a referee, and then he realized he really should mow his lawn. Someday he would write that novel.

Good intentions, bad follow-through. By now I suspect you're catching on to the point I'm making here.

We're approaching the end of our exploration of 1440 minutes in each day and the power contained in every one of those minutes. Sure, it's normal to let those moments slip by. It's normal to get up, rush to work, labor all day, come home tired, eat, watch TV, go to bed, and repeat. We may make some resolutions and devise a few dreams, but there just isn't time to do anything about them. Someday, we tell ourselves wistfully, we'll take a first step.

Another 1440 minutes drift by and we're another 1440 minutes closer to the end of our lives.

WHY BE NORMAL?

If the scenarios above are *normal* for most people, then here's where being *abnormal* is a far better choice. Why settle for a humdrum drift of time when we can consciously, intentionally invest our 1440 minutes to better our lives and the world we live in? Yes, of course we need to work. And sleep. And eat. And relax. And make resolutions and dream dreams.

But here's the difference, a life-changing difference.

What if we were to invest just ten to thirty minutes a day or perhaps ninety minutes one evening or Saturday per week to take actual, tangible steps toward making a resolution, goal, or dream come true?

What if today we focused 100 percent of our energy—even for just a portion of our 1440 minutes—on finally taking a *solid step* toward that big ambition that's been calling us?

What if we invested just 10 minutes a day in giving back, paying it forward, or blessing someone who just may need an act of kindness or a word of encouragement?

What if we gave 30 of our 1440 minutes to play with our children or help a neighbor? Or 60 minutes to volunteer at our church or in the community?

It seems like a small investment, but it could just be the beginning of something extraordinary.

All of these what-ifs don't have to be relegated to the category of "maybe someday," "when I feel inspired," "I'd like to but." Your dream can become reality. The time is now to begin to make that happen.

THE FIRST STEP

What we're talking about here is the importance of not only choosing and clarifying a dream but of taking actual steps to make the dream become reality. As we saw with Melanie and Jeff, that first step is often the hardest. But there's a classic saying you and I should keep in mind:

A journey of a thousand miles
begins with a single step.[1]

We won't complete a thousand miles or even one mile without intentionally taking that first decisive, pivotal step.

Take the first step and the second becomes a little easier to envision and execute. Then take the third step, followed by the fourth and fifth, and the journey toward fulfillment begins to take shape. Whatever your dream or resolution, its beginning can be small enough and manageable enough to fit into a single day. Whether it's 10 minutes, 20 minutes, or 30 minutes, step one will definitely fit into your 1440 minutes.

Choose, prioritize, decide, resolve, and take that first step. Think only of that first step, not of the miles ahead. Don't even think of the next step until today's single step is completed.

What are you going to do and do well *today*?

STEP ONE VENTURED

I know several people who lost their excess weight and got into fighting trim by walking and lifting weights just fifteen to thirty minutes a day. A few simply skipped the elevator at work and took the stairs. They reported much-improved blood pressure, energy, outlook, and sleep. But they each had to step out for that first brief walk and kneel over to hoist that first weight. They each had to take that first single step!

John Grisham wrote his first novel, *A Time to Kill*, by getting up at 5:30 each morning and writing a few hundred words before he left for work. He no longer has to go to another job.[2] But for that first novel he had to take the first step. He had to begin! Then his next days became a little easier and a little easier as his momentum increased. Today, Grisham still writes a book a year, and millions of sales later, he devotes most of his royalties to charities. But once upon a time he had to take that first step.

It takes courage. It takes tenacity. It takes commitment. But the power of the first step is just as available to Jeff and Melanie and to you and me as it is to those who start and who succeed.

YOU HAVE THE TIME

What is your resolution? Your dream? Your goal?

Whatever your God-inspired conviction or ambition, he has given you the time. Step one takes just a few minutes, so it definitely fits into your 1440-minute allotment for the day.

Throughout the day—this day—you *can* move toward your dream and accomplish it.

Don't be normal, my friend. Choose wisely. Make your dream your priority and go for it. Your journey begins with a single step.

But that single step can change your life.

TWENTY-FIVE

BAD DAY, GOOD HEART

Even if today is less than ideal,
your attitude can be real.

As I write this chapter, our world is embroiled in fear and uncertainty amid the 2020 COVID-19 pandemic. During the early weeks of the crisis, people of all ages were diagnosed as positive, thousands died, state governments shuttered restaurants and coffeehouses, millions of employees were sent home to work in isolation or self-quarantine, sporting events and concerts were canceled, and even churches held their services and group activities online.

While most media outlets displayed the frightful possibilities for disaster, it wasn't long before panic-fueled hoarding began. Soon there were shortages of vital home supplies such as toilet paper, facial tissue, and disposable diapers. Panic selling brought near-unprecedented losses to hard-saved 401(k)s and other long-term investments. Many adults reflected that, emotionally, the COVID-19 pandemic felt similar to the surreal days after America's 9/11 terrorist attacks.

THE CHOICE

But in the midst of what many dubbed the crazy days of the rampant virus, there were also millions of people who made the deliberate choice *not* to panic. I'm not talking about those irresponsible people who chose to ignore danger so they could party the nights away during their spring breaks at the beach. Rather, I regard with admiration those who, while being careful and responsible during the crisis, determined not to panic, not to believe the worst, not to hoard food or supplies at the expense of others, and not to sell off their investments during the panic-induced downward market spiral.

The wise folks I'm talking about chose to be bigger than the bad days. They may not have liked what was happening—and even felt justified fear—but they exercised their power of choice: *the power to choose hope over hopelessness, calm over chaos, and faith in the midst of fear.*

Fear exclaims, "It's a pandemic! Hunker down!"

Faith says, "How can I help my family be careful but also be of help to those around me?"

Fear screams, "I need to buy up every spare square of toilet paper!"

Faith says, "I'll try to find what I need, but I won't hoard. My neighbor needs it as much as I do."

Fear screeches, "How will we ever get through this?!"

Faith asserts, "This, too, shall pass."

In short, fear riles, while faith calms. Fear discourages, faith encourages. Fear dwells on what's going wrong, while faith focuses on how we can work together to help things go right.

What I observed during the coronavirus crisis was this: *faith keeps you anchored in every season every time.*

Faith says, "We will get through this together."

Those men and women and families who anchored their hope and faith in Jesus were much stronger—physically, mentally, and emotionally—than those who bought into the panic. They chose the calm amid the storm.

It was a choice during the pandemic, and it's a choice you and I have today and every day.

CHOOSING WISELY

Chances are good that, as you read this, the hard-hitting coronavirus will have run its course. But perhaps some other crisis has moved in to take its place. Could be another huge problem, or maybe you're just experiencing a crazy, hectic week.

Yes, life is tough. So what kind of attitude are you going to take into your next task, your next meeting, your next day?

The choice is yours. But please choose wisely.

In today's loudly cynical culture, it's so easy for us to default to the negative, to echo the disillusioned worldview all around us. It's also far too convenient for another cynical voice—that of the Devil himself—to whisper sweet nothings in our ears: "You're nothing. Your life stinks. It's all unfair. And while I've got your attention, you're ugly too. Obviously God doesn't love you. Never did."

Listen to those voices and you'll take a downward spiral into that next task, next meeting, next day. Fear, negativity, and cynicism produce a bad attitude. Then, to paraphrase Murphy's Law, if anything else can possibly go wrong, it will. A bad attitude almost guarantees that.

Our alternative, of course, is to overrule cynicism, negate negativity, and counter evil lies.

Remember, we do this by intentionally choosing faith over fear, even when things don't look so promising at the moment.

GOD'S WAY THROUGH THE TOUGH MOMENTS

I'm blessed to confirm that you and I have an incredible array of rock-solid promises from which to draw strength and counsel: the Word of our loving Creator himself.

Soak these remarkably relevant verses into your mind and spirit. Pick two or three favorites, write them down, and place them where you'll see them when you need an attitude boost. Claim them for that tough task, contentious meeting, or challenging day ahead.

- "'For I know the plans I have for you,' declares the LORD, 'plans to prosper you and not to harm you, plans to give you hope and a future.'" (Jer. 29:11)
- "Do not fear, for I am with you. Do not anxiously look about you, for I am your God. I will strengthen you, surely I will help you, surely I will uphold you with My righteous right hand." (Isa. 41:10 NASB)
- "Trust in the LORD with all your heart and lean not on your own understanding; in all your ways submit to him, and he will make your paths straight." (Prov. 3:5–6)
- "Do not be anxious about anything, but in every situation, by prayer and petition, with thanksgiving, present your requests to God. And the peace of God, which transcends all understanding, will guard your hearts and your minds in Christ Jesus." (Phil. 4:6–7)
- "And my God will supply all your needs according to His riches in glory in Christ Jesus." (Phil. 4:19 NASB)
- "For God has not given us a spirit of fear, but of power and of love and of a sound mind." (2 Tim. 1:7 NKJV)

We can, indeed, counter a bad day with a good attitude. We develop and keep that good attitude by choosing wisely and deliberately between cultural cynicism and trust in God's Word.

Then, whether we're facing a pandemic or just a tough meeting, we can take on the day with faith (not fear), hope (not hopelessness), and calm (not chaos).

People will be drawn to that and will be inspired to pass it along.

TWENTY-SIX

MASTER OF ONE

Greatness flows out of excellence,
no matter how small the task.

It's Super Bowl Sunday. Your favorite team has made it to the championship. Friends and family are crowded into your living room around the TV, but no one pays attention to the snack trays or beverages.

That's because it's the fourth quarter, and the game clock has just dipped under a minute to go. Your team is down by four points and has the ball. It's crunch time: fourth down and the ball is thirty yards from the end zone. The whole season comes down to this.

The players break the huddle and calmly take their places at the line of scrimmage. The quarterback takes the snap and drifts back a few yards while the receivers run their routes. He dodges a defensive player, then another, and he steps up, firing the ball high into the air. The ball floats as if carried by invisible hands over a defender's shoulder and into a receiver's hands. For a moment, time stands still until chaos erupts as you realize they've done it.

Touchdown!

Even if football is not your thing and all that sounded like a foreign language, you can appreciate the beauty of the moment. With one *excellent* throw and one *excellent* catch the victory is theirs.

At least that's how the sportswriters and commentators will likely describe the play. As if one moment contains the whole victory.

I propose a different perspective, one that promises a powerful payoff in our quest for maximum opportunity and abundance in every one of our 1440 minutes each day.

If I were to write the article the next day describing the game-winning play, I'd say the pass and the catch were *successful*. They got the job done and fulfilled the goal the team had pursued all year. But they were not *excellent*. I would reserve that word for something else, namely, a masterful way of life that too few of us reach for, much less attain.

Think of it this way: if the poise, focus, athleticism, and skill necessary to complete the play and win the game are the ripened fruit of success, then excellence is the tree on which they grow. Success often manifests in a single moment; excellence must be present in every moment all along the way. Success makes the highlight reels on TV; excellence often goes unnoticed. In fact, the truest expression of excellence on the football field in my illustration may be found in the other players out of range of the camera's eye: a lineman blocking well away from the ball, an assistant coach giving 110 percent, an equipment manager staying late until every task is done, an accountant working diligently in the front office.

Furthermore, it is possible to achieve success without excellence and to practice excellence without the kind of success that draws attention. The school janitor who works alone into the night to make sure the students return to the cleanest, safest environment possible embodies excellence. The salesman who spends so much time surfing the internet at the office and meeting his quotas with innate telephone charm has achieved a certain success but little excellence.

To drive home the point: excellence and success are not the same thing.

THE EXTRA MILE, EVERY TIME

Why is that so important to us? Because we live in a culture that too often honors the fruit and not the tree. If you decide to be successful, you could easily start to pursue only what's profitable and gratifying. Excellence, by its nature, seeks the best for everyone: teammates, family members, coworkers, customers, the baristas who serve your coffee, and the people who pick up your trash every week. It exemplifies the mindset we've been working to achieve throughout this book.

Here are some key concepts to seeking and developing excellence.

EXCELLENCE INVOLVES PREPARATION

Just as Olympians train diligently for many years, making countless sacrifices and relentlessly focusing on their goals, so can we form habits that will lead to excellence. We can condition our minds, hearts, and bodies to move beyond mediocrity and toward distinction. Moments arrive every day that provide opportunities to use your training and call upon the habits you have put in place.

The Greek philosopher Aristotle said, "We are what we repeatedly do. Excellence, then, is not an act, but a habit."[1] We can develop many helpful habits, such as maintaining a morning routine, following a daily schedule, giving generously, reading for at least thirty minutes every day, and setting aside regular times for spiritual guidance.

Excellence materializes the moment you decide to do your best and draw upon your existing resources, which you have been developing over time. This is the opportunity packed into every one of the 1440 minutes God gave you today. Seize it and transformation follows.[2]

EXCELLENCE IS NOT ABOUT BEING PERFECT

People who practice excellence in all they do can still fail at their specific goals. The quarterback and receiver in our Super Bowl example might have approached every moment of the season with a solid commitment to excellence in all the little tasks of playing well and still could have dropped the ball and lost the game. Then their love of excellence would push them to show up the next day ready to get back to work to be even better. *Better*, not perfect.

EXCELLENCE IS IN THE (SEEMINGLY) SMALL OFFERINGS YOU MAKE TO OTHERS

I knew a woman whose job was to deliver meals to a dozen elderly people in her community on Mondays, Wednesdays, and Fridays. Thirty-six times every week she took the time to write a personal note to include in the package. She was an artist and would doodle a drawing on the page or include a fragment of a poem or a Bible verse.

The program was designed to meet nutritional needs, but my friend's commitment to excellence led her to deliver so much more than that. She brought a loving and life-giving message to those folks along with the food: *someone still cares for you*. As you might expect, these personal notes eventually led to personal relationships between the note writer and the recipients. A surprising act of kindness evolved into genuine friendships.

EXCELLENCE DOESN'T WAIT FOR SOMEONE ELSE TO FIX WHAT'S BROKEN OR CLEAN UP WHAT'S MESSY

The person who lives by excellence takes responsibility for making his or her corner of the world better, the best it can be, every day. The only advantage they seek is the pleasure of living in that world and seeing others enjoy it too.

EXCELLENCE IS ITS OWN REWARD

The thrill of winning is nothing compared to the satisfaction of ending each day certain you've done your best or the excitement of waking up to 1440 new opportunities for quiet greatness. Form the excellence habit today, and I guarantee you'll soon lose your taste for mediocrity!

The apostle Paul called each of us "God's handiwork, created in Christ Jesus to do good works, which God prepared in advance for us to do" (Eph. 2:10). He also said, "Do you not know that in a race all the runners run, but only one gets the prize? Run in such a way as to get the prize. Everyone who competes in the games goes into strict training. They do it to get a crown that will not last, but we do it to get a crown that will last forever" (1 Cor. 9:24–25).

Give your best. Do your best. Be your best. In times of trouble and when all is well. Practice excellence when no one is looking, when it costs you something, when you are tired or broke or in a bad mood. Be better today than yesterday, and be ready for the next step up tomorrow. An excellent life is both your calling and your inheritance. Pursue it with all of your energy and tenacity each day.

TWENTY-SEVEN

MIRACULOUS DISASTER

If you're weighed down by too much stuff, lighten your load.

There's no getting around it.

We Americans really like our stuff.

We collect stuff for all seasons and every eventuality: lawn mowers, snowblowers, Christmas decorations, Halloween accessories, bicycles no one rides, exercise machines no one uses, plastic gizmos whose origin and purpose no one remembers, boxes that haven't been opened since the last family move. There are closets and drawers full of free-floating things that somehow feel necessary, even if it's been years since we used them.

I have a garage full of collectibles that I tell myself I am going to sort through and pare down someday. But it's a telltale sign the things have been in the garage way too long when my collectibles start to collect things themselves.

It's not enough to stuff our houses and garages and sheds with stuff. As of early 2020, Americans were spending $39 billion a year to rent 1.7 billion square feet of self-storage space to handle the overflow.[1] Garage sales only move the stuff from one household to another. Once the merry-go-round stops, bloated landfills are left holding the (trash) bag. We call our stuff "wealth" and count ourselves lucky compared to people in other societies who have fewer possessions.

And we're wrong about that.

Okay, not *entirely* wrong. A certain level of material comfort and security is good, and there's nothing wrong with wanting nice things. Contrary to what some believe, poverty is not some exalted spiritual state we should aspire to.

But here's the key question: What is the cutoff point? How do you know when you've gone too far and your stuff has stopped being beneficial and has become burdensome instead? I gained some insight into one way to answer that question the day my family lost everything.

PROOF OF NECESSITY

It was a beautiful July evening. I had just finished a long week of travel and was finally back home. The first stop I made was my mother's house. As I got out of the car, a light breeze carried the hint of fresh, crisp air, and the sinking sun washed everything in yellows and golds.

I walked into the house and saw my mother was cooking. She was preparing a spread from scratch. Mom was tossing a salad with vinaigrette as I approached, and the bread smelled like it had just come out of the oven. Cooking dinner was always a joy for my mom, almost like a minivacation for her.

We all sat down at the table, and as she dished out the food, we fell instantly into easy and familiar conversation, talking about all kinds of things.

Although the food tasted wonderfully familiar, I noticed how different the décor and design of the kitchen was compared to the kitchen we'd been sitting in the year before. Her old house—the dream house my father built before he passed—had been consumed in a fire, along with everything they owned. The fire had been caused by a freak accident; a propane tank exploded on the side of the house, and all of our family members were inside. Thank God we got out in time, but we escaped with nothing but the clothes on our backs!

At first, the loss was unfathomable. Heirloom furniture, family mementos, keepsakes, and a lifelong accumulation of possessions were reduced to ashes. In the aftermath, my mother rented a smaller home and furnished it with the bare minimums she needed to get by.

The day her insurance settlement check arrived, something astonishing happened.

"I don't want it all back," Mom said. "A few weeks of being forced to live more simply has made me realize how much lighter and happier I feel."

Rather than rebuild a home the same size as her previous one, she chose to reboot her life. She decided to start with nothing and add only what proved to be necessary. Turns out, that was a lot less than she ever imagined.

She didn't need to tell me that one payoff of that bold decision was greater contentment and presence in each moment. I could see that for myself.

LIGHTING A (FIGURATIVE) FIRE IN YOUR LIFE

The process my mother went through is well known: *minimalism*.[2] Lots of people have reached the same conclusion: too much stuff takes a heavy toll on our ability to relax and enjoy life as it is right now. I would add that material excess reduces our availability to the opportunities for spontaneous greatness in every moment. Paring down, shedding weight, lightening your load is a great way to get that back.

Here are four reasons why.

LESS STUFF MEANS LESS WORK TO PAY FOR IT

We're all used to calculating the value of what we own in dollars. Forget that. Instead, mentally price things in the number of *hours* you will spend working to earn the dollars to buy it. Hours that could be better invested in much more profitable things.

Henry David Thoreau wrote, "There is no more fatal blunderer than he who consumes the greater part of his life getting his living."[3] Whenever possible, choose time over stuff.

LESS STUFF MEANS MORE SPACE FOR YOU

Researchers have amassed a lot of evidence to support the idea that a crowded, cluttered environment is bad for you.[4] Living in a messy home has a negative effect on everything from your eating and sleeping habits to your mental health and cognitive performance. Getting rid of excess stuff will make room to move, breathe, think, play, and live more abundantly than ever before.

LESS STUFF FREES UP THE TIME YOU SPENT TAKING CARE OF IT

People with children wear a lot of hats: doctor, counselor, food service worker, sanitation engineer. One that's often overlooked is home repair specialist, that is, one who fixes a seemingly endless stream of broken things. You know who you are. You know what I'm saying.

But even without children in the house, stuff you maintain or repair today seems to get right back in line for another repair later on. You can reclaim that time and effort by reducing the population of things clamoring for it.

LESS STUFF MEANS LESS WORRY OVER WHAT HAPPENS TO IT

How much heartburn do you incur wondering whether your insurance policies are sufficient to cover your stuff in the event of a fire, burglary, tornado, flood, asteroid strike? Do you tense up when the neighborhood kids are playing with too much enthusiasm in a room full of your stuff? Would you like to stop? Cut down on your stuff and cut down on your worries.

Let us be guided by the words of Jesus:

> If God cares so wonderfully for wildflowers that are here today and thrown into the fire tomorrow, he will certainly care for you. Why do you have so little faith?
>
> So don't worry about these things, saying, "What will we eat? What will we drink? What will we wear?" These things dominate the thoughts of unbelievers, but your heavenly Father already knows all your needs. Seek the Kingdom of God above all else, and live righteously, and he will give you everything you need. (Matt. 6:30–33 NLT)

Cash in some of your priceless minutes today by lightening your load and your life. You don't need a fire or a disaster to carry away everything that's weighing you down and holding you back. Use the time, energy, money, and enthusiasm you gain to get busy creating *real* wealth, the kind that doesn't crumble, burn, or fade.

FOOD INSPECTOR

What goes into your heart comes out in your life.

We all know eating too much junk food is bad for us in many ways. Poor eating habits eventually lead to damaging health conditions, such as diabetes, high blood pressure, high cholesterol, and a long list of other ailments.

But as bad as junk food is for our health, we eat it anyway! Why? Because we love how it tastes!

Our spiritual life is a lot like our daily diet. Just as we replace fruits, veggies, and whole grains with soda, candy, and chips, we often substitute spiritual food—prayer, Scripture, worshiping in a local church community—with the junk food that distracts us from godly living and thinking. We find ourselves too busy for daily talks with God and immersion in his Word, skipping church to sleep in and watch football, and then we wonder why we feel soul-sick. We feel depressed, frustrated, irritable, and anxious. Rather than filling our lives with soul food that brings genuine contentment and inspiration, we consume junk food that leaves us feeling empty and dissatisfied.

To fully utilize the 1440 minutes of our day, we need to monitor what we are putting into our heart, mind, and soul. To make each minute meaningful, we must fill ourselves with the daily bread that is fortifying, nourishing, and strengthening.

One of my annual rituals is to start each new year by fasting. Some years are relatively simple, relatively easy, perhaps eliminating food for a few days or cutting out just certain items from my diet. But some other years are more strenuous and severe, such as this year when I subsisted on only water for twenty-one days. After consulting with a physician to make sure this was safe, I stopped consuming food altogether and drank only H_2O (a gallon of it every day, or so it seemed).

At the beginning of every fast, I try to adjust my appetite. I eliminate food slowly but surely, so eventually I feel less desire and need to eat.

Two years ago my desire was to get leaner. I did not do a strict fast, eliminating food completely, but instead adjusted my diet. I reduced my carbohydrate intake and increased my protein consumption. The eating plan allowed me to change my daily actions, but it did not change my appetite. I consumed the same amount of food, just different types of food. I discovered that I kept eating and snacking—all according to the diet plan—but the new regimen was not as effective for me because my appetite remained the same.

This happens in our experience of daily living as well. To be most effective and to reach our potential, we must adjust our appetite, carefully monitoring what we desire and what we eat—consuming things that feed us and not just fill us.

In the Sermon on the Mount, Jesus said, "Blessed are those who hunger and thirst for righteousness, for they shall be satisfied" (Matt. 5:6 ESV). I like how Eugene Peterson phrased this statement: "You're blessed when you've worked up a good appetite for God. He's food and drink in the best meal you'll ever eat" (MSG).

Let's carefully examine what we hunger and thirst for and how we seek to satisfy our appetite, both physical and spiritual. Doing so will help us make the most of *this day* and every day.

BECOME A DIET DETECTIVE

When going on a diet, it's important to recognize our weakness. Is it soda, chocolate, fried foods? We can't eliminate the empty calories until we figure out where they're coming from. What do we reach for in our moments of weakness, our times of sadness, or out of habit and convenience? Once we identify the junk and cut it out, we'll find ourselves with a big gap in our menu and dinner planning. Will we replace junk with more junk, or will we turn to what's healthy and wholesome?

When it comes to our spiritual life, we must identify what's taking us from the walk with God we desire. Perhaps it's pornography or greed or a secret dependency on alcohol or prescription pills. Whatever the harmful issue, we have to recognize and name it before we can eliminate it from our life. And once it's cut, we have to fill the void with something good, something healthy for our spirit and soul.

Many people diet and achieve success only to succumb to temptation, craving, and convenience. This can cause guilt, anger, and shame. We wanted to do better. We tried hard, but failure and junk fillers found us again.

We might be afraid we'll do the same thing spiritually once we begin living the life God wants for us. It's all too easy to fall into old habits, especially when we are bombarded with ways to find more and more junk to fill our souls. We might be afraid others will see us as hypocritical. We might be afraid our spouse or a friend will say, "I knew you couldn't stick with it! You'll never change."

Repentance is our action, and forgiveness is God's reaction out of his perfect love for us. So while it's true that no one is perfect, it's important to remember that God is the King of second chances. Our power to live fully today comes from the power of God to fill us with his Spirit and strength.

WHAT ARE YOU HUNGRY FOR?

The majority of Americans don't experience physical hunger and thirst. Being hungry is missing breakfast and having to wait until lunch, and being thirsty is craving anything other than water. No big deal, really, and we can usually identify it and know just what we'd like to fill that hunger with.

Each and every one of us has a spiritual hunger, but sometimes we can't pinpoint exactly what it is or how to meet the need. So we use phrases such as

"Something is missing from my life."
"I'm burned out."
"There has to be more to life than this."
"Something just isn't right."

Even when it seems the cards are falling in our favor and great things are happening, there is still a nagging sensation that something's missing.

Why is it that so many people feel empty and unsatisfied? Scripture says it's because they're looking for solutions in the wrong places.

PLEASURE

The first place we normally look to be satisfied is in pleasures.

If I could go on vacation . . .
If I could travel the world . . .
If I could have a spa day . . .

The writer of Ecclesiastes tells us, "No matter how much we see, we are never satisfied; no matter how much we hear, we are not content" (1:8 TLB). We find this to be true when we get up in the middle of the night to forage for something satisfying. We don't know exactly what we want; we just know we want something. So we open the refrigerator door, take a bite of an old sandwich, nibble on a slice of cake, and then head back to bed, still unsatisfied.

Many people are the same way in life, searching for something that will bring satisfaction and fill an empty place inside. They'll go for what is convenient, accessible, and immediate. Jesus told us of the kind of sustenance that truly satisfies: "But whoever drinks of the water that I will give him will never be thirsty again. The water that I will give him will become in him a spring of water welling up to eternal life" (John 4:14 ESV).

ACHIEVEMENTS

There is a myth that says success produces satisfaction. But clearly that's not true. Many successful people are unsatisfied. After many accomplishments and winning at nearly everything, there is an emptiness, a feeling that something's just not right.

The Bible says, "Everyone's toil is for their mouth, yet their appetite is never satisfied" (Eccl. 6:7). There are a lot of busy people who achieve many things, just not things of lasting value. We can avoid being one of them by deciding we will no longer occupy ourselves with activities that don't really matter, but instead we will invest each of our 1440 daily minutes in pursuits and people in a meaningful way.

POSSESSIONS AND WEALTH

We see the words "Satisfaction Guaranteed" on products quite frequently these days. But are people truly *guaranteed* to be satisfied? Of course not! The Bible states, "He who loves money shall never have enough. The foolishness of thinking that wealth brings happiness!" (Eccl. 5:10 TLB).

No matter what our society tells us, money is not the answer to happiness. Consider, for instance, the story of Emanuel Ninger, an exceptionally talented artist of the late 1800s. He was arrested for counterfeiting (he specialized in fifty-dollar bills). His counterfeit money fooled nearly everyone, but he was caught when he attempted to pay a bar tab and a bartender noticed the ink begin to run when the bill was wet. At the same time, as an artist, Ninger had created three portraits, each of which sold for more than $5,000 (which would be a fortune in today's money).

Ninger had an amazing talent, one that could have made him wealthy. This was a God-given gift, but Ninger let his good gift go bad. Instead of earning riches by creating beautiful artwork, he spent countless hours handcrafting faulty phony money that landed him in jail.[1]

Likewise, the quality of our decisions will determine the quality of our destiny. And if we're letting money and material things determine our daily actions, we'll find that we are never quite satisfied with anything.

What, then, is the secret of satisfaction? The Bible says, "Take delight in the LORD, and he will give you the desires of your heart" (Ps. 37:4).

Happiness and satisfaction are byproducts of seeking and delighting in God. But if we try to satisfy our soul hunger with wealth and possessions, we are bound to be disappointed. We need a constant reminder that the good life isn't about accumulating more goods. Instead, it comes from the One who *is good*. When we fill our lives with the good things of God—his love, grace, and truth—we will come to know what real fulfillment is.

THE WHY AND WHAT OF JUNK

We all have access to God's wisdom through prayer, Scripture reading, and the act of listening for his guidance. When we use these powerful resources, we can ask that our eyes be opened to the junk we're feeding ourselves. We can ask that God help us change our ways and begin filling our hearts and souls with righteousness.

The first step is probably the hardest: calling out the *what* and *why* of the junk that goes into our hearts and minds. It isn't easy to take a personal inventory and identify what's junk and where it came from. It starts with being honest with ourselves.

- What do you long for?
- What do you reach for when you're sad or feeling bad? What numbs the pain?
- How do you go about getting those things?
- Do you find yourself defending your actions?
- Do you ask God to have things your way, right away, or do you ask him to do his work in you?

The answers to these questions will reveal what you're filling your life with.

If you've been loading up on junk for far too long, you may feel too soul-sick to even think about changing your habits. It's certainly easier to throw up your hands than it is to roll up your sleeves to engage in introspection and listen to God. I'm betting there are a few thoughts running through your head that you want to use as excuses not to do this hard work. Here are two that cross my mind often.

WE'RE AFRAID WE'RE TOO MESSED UP FOR GOD TO FIX

The good news is that God accepts us and loves us exactly as we are while he is calling us to fulfill our potential through godly living and thinking. Grace abounds no less for us than for others. Getting right with God stirs up a desire from somewhere deep inside to follow his ways and live with purpose every minute. It's the junk of the world, combined with human nature, that keeps us from following that desire. And when that desire is misguided or lacking, so too is our life.

Finding fulfillment comes from being content right where we are with just what we've got. If we let him, God will continue to fill us up with so much good and abundance that it will crowd out all those other things we've been consuming over the years.

WE'RE AFRAID WE'RE STUCK WITH WHAT WE'VE GOT

Like many people, I enjoy the convenience of shopping online. Once, many years ago, I excitedly ordered an expensive electronic device from eBay. This was back when eBay lacked certain safeguards and every transaction had a "buyer beware" warning. Nonetheless, I took my chances and ordered the gadget.

As the days passed I looked forward more and more to its arrival. But after two weeks, it hadn't shown up. I emailed the seller, who responded by sending me the tracking number. I followed the tracking, but the package had yet to arrive. Finally, after three weeks, the package was in my mailbox. I immediately tore open the box, right there in the doorway. After wrestling with the tape and packaging, I looked inside and found a couple of bricks and a towel.

I hurried to my computer and emailed the seller, who pointed out that the terms of sale stipulated absolutely *no* returns or refunds for any reason. He had tricked me by giving me something I didn't ask for, didn't want, and hadn't bargained for. And worse, there was nothing I could do to fix it.

In life we often receive things that don't really belong to us and aren't what we asked for, wanted, or bargained for. These things often come from the Enemy, but sometimes we fail to see that. Instead, we take on the thing as if it actually belongs to us, no returns or refunds allowed.

Thankfully, this isn't how it works with God. He has empowered us to reject these unwanted packages, to put them right back in the mailbox, mark the package "Return to Sender," and never have to see them again. It's up to you. Will you hold on to the junk the Enemy has forced into your life, or will you label it "Return to Sender" at the first chance you get?

It's true that no one is perfect, but as a child of God you have the strength to fight temptation and stay focused on healthy living. You have the tools—prayer, the Bible, church, community—to help you live fully and send back to the Enemy all the sneaky ways he tries to bring you down.

It's seldom that radical change occurs overnight. You're going to have to do a lot of hard work and go through some struggles before you get to the place you want to be, namely, living the good life 1440 minutes of each day. You can live every day with maximum contentment and influence because these words apply to you: "I can do all this through him who gives me strength" (Phil. 4:13). That means it's possible for you to exchange your old soul diet for one that is healthy, nutritious, and virtuous and leads to fullness and strength.

TWENTY-NINE

WAIT TRAINING

A seed can be planted in a minute,
but the harvest takes time.

Let's admit it: most of us aren't very good at waiting. We want what we want *when* we want it. Who can blame us, considering all the time pressures we live under these days? Minutes are precious commodities to be spent accomplishing tasks, pursuing goals, or checking off to-do list items.

Yet when it comes to the hope we place in God's promises, impatience can gum up the project in a hurry. It isn't that God delights in making us wait for our own good. Some things just can't be rushed, no matter how badly we wish otherwise. The truth is, we probably wouldn't like the result if our wish were suddenly granted.

When it comes to the necessity of waiting and the value of patience, I love the imagery of planting a garden. After all, no one has ever planted a seed and harvested a crop the same day. If that's what you expect, you are doomed to disappointment. When I plant a pack of seeds for an herb garden, my three-year-old son might expect to see the fully grown plants standing tall in the soil the very next day. But it would be ridiculous for me to expect herbs to be ready that fast. No matter how hard I watch the pot and how much I want those herbs in my spaghetti sauce, it's not going to happen overnight. It's going to take time.

Everything in God's creation is in constant motion and follows a path. The process of moving from one state to another is just that, a process. There is always a period of time between planting crops and the emergence of green shoots when the field still looks barren. Hope seems like a foolish fantasy. Based solely on appearance, despair might seem a reasonable conclusion. But it's always a misguided one.

If you've planted the seed, the harvest is coming in its own perfect time.

It is no wonder that Scripture is full of references to planting, cultivating, sowing, and reaping. The poetic language of fruitfulness and the bountiful harvest occurs again and again in God's Word. It beautifully conveys the essence of his promise to us of abundant and joyful life. "For the LORD comforts Zion; he comforts all her waste places and makes her wilderness like Eden, her desert like the garden of the LORD; joy and gladness will be found in her, thanksgiving and the voice of song" (Isa. 51:3 ESV).

That is the treasure that waits for us in each of our 1440 minutes each day! And an understanding of growing things helps us to embrace this promise.

WHAT A GARDENER KNOWS

Let's pause a minute and consider a fundamental but often-overlooked element in all that pastoral imagery: *patience.* It's what separates true wisdom from mere wishful thinking. Bookstore shelves are full of titles that offer the secrets to having everything your heart could desire *right now!*

God's way is slower and steadier than that. How do we know? Because an instant harvest is not found anywhere in the natural world he created. It certainly isn't the way things work on a farm or in a backyard garden. It is true that the promise of a rich harvest is *set in motion* the instant a person plants a seed. But between planting and picking lies a wonderful process that must be followed. This fact requires us to be in relationship with the earth—listening, guarding, touching, and loving it. It requires us to be *present*.

The same wisdom applies to everything we hope to nurture and grow in our lives, to all we've set out to achieve in this book. To help us to embrace it and make it our own, here are six things a gardener knows to do and cultivates the patience to do them all.

A GARDENER PREPARES THE SOIL

A plot of land that is too hard or dry, too choked with weeds, or depleted of nutrients will yield little but disappointment. Before a single seed comes out of the bag for planting, the wise gardener makes an honest assessment of the ground. Is it as healthy as it needs to be to nourish the planned crop? Where is it lacking and why? The gardener uses this survey to identify and correct problems that might rob her of success before she even begins.

For us, that means taking stock of the soil of our habits, hearts, and minds when we set out to achieve greatness in every moment. Are there weeds that need pulling? Do it! Our harvest of abundance and joy depends on it.

A GARDENER CHOOSES THE RIGHT SEED

Obviously, there is no sense planting turnips if we hope to harvest tomatoes. But this principle can be more subtle than that. Tomatoes come in many varieties. Some will thrive in the garden plot we have prepared, others will not. Some go great on a ham sandwich while others make better salsa and pasta sauce.

Here's the point: make sure you know precisely what you want in your life before you plant, and selectively choose your opportunities with those goals in mind.

A GARDENER KNOWS WHEN TO PLANT

Solomon wrote, "For everything there is a season, and a time for every matter under heaven: . . . a time to plant, and a time to pluck up what is planted" (Eccl. 3:1–2 ESV).

Timing is everything. Plant too soon and the seeds will freeze and not sprout, too late and they'll wither in the heat. Being in relationship with the earth, a good gardener reads the signs of the season and acts only when the right moment arrives. This takes a proper mix of patience while waiting and action when the time is right.

The key lesson for us: be present and listen. When the time is right to seize opportunity and act, we'll know it.

A GARDENER BELIEVES IN THE PLANT BEFORE IT APPEARS

For the gardener, every spring is a refresher course in living by faith, not by sight. That's because once the seed is covered over with soil, nothing happens that can be seen. For days and even weeks it appears she has wasted her time. The temptation to poke into beds and verify things are moving along—or even start over entirely—can be overwhelming. But experience has taught her to have faith. She has done her part and knows to let God do his.

A GARDENER PROTECTS THE YOUNG PLANT FROM HARM

Once the shoot appears, the gardener settles into a long season of consistent, painstaking nurture. She invests many hours watering her plants (but not too much), shades them, pulls weeds away from them, feeds them with fertilizer, and battles the bugs that want an early harvest of their own, long before the payoff is remotely at hand. After a hailstorm, she cleans up the damage. On a cold night, she shields the plants from frost.

In other words, between the visionary act of planting a seed in your life and reaping the reward, there often lies a long stretch of thankless *work*. Skip that part, and you'll never know what might have been come harvest time.

A GARDENER HARVESTS ONLY IN SEASON

Somewhere along the way, blossoms appear, followed by developing fruit. Until then, the gardener has tended only the vines. Now she can see the beans, slender and green and enticing. Every day they grow and look more and more like the food she set out to enjoy. But she knows better. Picked too soon (or too late), her vegetables will certainly disappoint and might not be edible at all. With patience and discernment she will wait for the sweet spot of *ripeness*.

When you have carefully tended a dream, stay present and aware to know when to reap the reward.

Never forget, the real bounty is in the treasure you can store in heaven. *That* is always worth the wait.

THIRTY

THE MAGNIFICENT MAP

Cartographers draw the world as it is. Spend today charting the world you hope to create.

I love looking at old maps. In the faded ink you can almost feel the courage and sense of adventure it took to gaze beyond the horizon and divine the shape of the unknown world. Every line on the parchment is a manifestation of mariner stories, detective work, and faith.

In many respects, books such as *The Power of 1440* are akin to the maps of old. When it comes to knowing how to live our best lives in the precious minutes we are given, the horizon still marks the edge of mystery. There are no satellites in orbit to triangulate the truth, so we must do our best to gather clues and assemble them into a vision of what's waiting for us out there. On this journey we are all adventurers, searching for new worlds of opportunity and abundance. I've done my best to show the way as I see it. Now, it's time to chart your own course forward.

What do you do with all the information contained in this map of 1440? How do you carry on? First, consider that all maps have limitations, which wise explorers keep in mind. Here are some to consider about the map you've just read.

MAPS SEE THE WORLD THROUGH SOMEONE ELSE'S EYES

During the age of discovery, when brave people set out to explore the unknown, mapmakers mostly waited onshore for them to return with their ship's logs packed with stories and crude measurements. Even those who went to sea themselves could not avoid filtering what they observed through their own biases and assumptions. Whether an explorer saw the lands on the horizon as the East Indies or an entirely new world generally depended on the beliefs he already held. Future captains held in their hands only a map of what its maker thought to be real.

That's also true of those who give well-meaning advice about how to live your life to the fullest. As you set out with such a map in hand, never forget it isn't meant as a set of rigid directions to be followed to the letter. I've made notes on my journey, detailing what I've seen and learned, but only in the hope that you would go there yourself and continue the exploration as only *you* can.

MAPS ARE NOT THE TERRAIN THEY REPRESENT

I read about an Inuit elder who had lived his entire life on a rocky island in the Arctic Circle in northern Canada. For nearly nine decades he had survived without modern technology or mechanized conveniences. He had followed the traditional practices handed down to him by his family and tribe and had little use for any new ways of being.

Visiting anthropologists took an interest in trying to see the world as he did—literally. They asked him to draw a map of a particularly complex stretch of coastline on the island, where the land folded and curved in numerous inlets, coves, and rocky points. Their own map, derived from satellite imagery, looked like a collection of jagged squiggles.

Puzzled by the request at first, the man eventually caught on to what they wanted. He sketched an outline of what he saw in his mind, drawing on a lifetime of memories. When he finished, the researchers overlaid the two maps and were astonished to see how remarkably similar they were. He had accurately recalled most of the detail and relative distances of the terrain. When they expressed to him how impressed they were by this feat, the elder laughed and told them both maps were a waste of paper. Intrigued, they asked him why.

"Does it say where the walrus are right now?" he replied. "Can a man paddle his boat against the tide along there? In summer, where does the moss grow best?"

For him, the landscape where he had grown up hunting, fishing, and gathering plants for food and medicine was *alive,* ever changing, bountiful, but also dangerous. His knowledge was rooted in personal experience and lifelong relationship. What could a flat line of ink tell anyone about any of that?

"I could draw my wife's face for you," the man said. "But would you know her?"

The truth is, if the researchers had asked *two* elders to draw a map of the island, the results might have looked the same, but their lived experiences would be very different.

Keep that in mind as you chart your future. The journey is yours and yours alone. Along the way you must take roads I never dreamed of, meet people with stories I've never heard, take in wonders that only you can see.

MAPS ARE FIXED

A map is meant to depict the world as it is now. That has its uses in the world of everyday business. When I order a pizza, I'm glad the delivery driver can easily find my house before the pizza gets cold, because the map shows him my address.

But here's the God-given opportunity we've been exploring throughout this book: the magnificent power to map your world as it *could* be. In that quest, we are not limited to what is or has been. We are free to create something new, to rewrite the rules that have held us back, and to shape a different future than we've imagined before.

Here's how to do that, starting right now.

BE BOLD

Now is not the time for excessive timidity. Dream *big*. God has made you the captain of your future life. You get to decide what you want the new world of abundance to look like, so don't hold back.

Think of it this way: the wind will blow and the currents will flow in whatever direction you choose. That's the power you've been given by the grace of God in Jesus. He showed us by example and by direct promise that we can design the landscape of our lives—with enough faith.

Jesus said, "Truly, I say to you, whoever says to this mountain, 'Be taken up and thrown into the sea,' and does not doubt in his heart, but believes that what he says will come to pass, it will be done for him" (Mark 11:23 ESV).

Believe it!

BE SPECIFIC

Don't say to yourself, "I want my life to be *better*." Take out as many pieces of paper as you need and make detailed lists of everything you want to have, be, and do. No one makes a shopping list that simply says "groceries." That much is obvious. What *exactly* do you want to eat? What's your meal plan?

ASK. SEEK. KNOCK.

Take the bold and specific map you've created to God. Right now and in every one of your 1440 minutes every day. "For everyone who asks receives, and the one who seeks finds, and to the one who knocks it will be opened" (Matt. 7:8 ESV).

The choice is yours. You can sit on the shore and chart the adventures of others or launch your own expedition into a new world. You have what it takes to make your own map, one that is bold, beautiful, and breathtaking. You have the courage, inspiration, and resources to chart a new course for your life that will lead you to opportunity and abundance. Like the prophet Isaiah, you will hear God tell you, "Forget the former things; do not dwell on the past. See, I am doing a new thing! Now it springs up; do you not perceive it? I am making a way in the wilderness and streams in the wasteland" (Isa. 43:18–19).

Each minute of each day you can step toward a future brimming with promise and possibilities.

NO TIME TO WASTE

When I was growing up, one of the things I most enjoyed was watching Chicago Bulls games with my dad. We watched obsessively. But more often than not, the games were at night, and my father wanted to make sure I got to bed on time. So he made me record all the games on our VHS recorder to watch and study, play by play, the next day.

When I went to school the following day, I didn't want my friends to give me any details about the game or tell me who won. I didn't want to know how things would end; that would spoil the game for me.

But in real life, we're just the opposite. We *want* to know the ending. We want to know how everything will play out in our lives and where, exactly, we will end up. God, however, gives us info on a need-to-know basis. If you ever read the story of Moses, you know that God gave Moses a forty-year wilderness plan but made him uncover and unpack each set of 1440 opportunities one by one.

In Psalm 119:105, God tells us that he will be a lamp unto our feet. If you've ever walked with a lamp, you know that a lamp illuminates only a step or two at a time. All you can see is the path immediately in front of you and no farther.

When times are tough and we're facing a mountain of trials, we can usually see only the immediacy of what's at hand. Even though God doesn't tell us in advance each and every step we're going to take on our life path, he *does* give us a promise to cling onto: he tells us that at the end of the situation or circumstance we're facing, with faith in Christ Jesus, *we win*.

Unlike the basketball games of my youth, in this life it's good to know the ending. I'm glad to know that despite the work of the Enemy, despite my adversities, even despite my failures and setbacks, I have hope. And so do you. The fact that you are still fighting is proof that the struggle has not overtaken you.

There are plenty of things that can consume our time and keep our focus off of enjoying life. We must remember that we are the ones who make the decision whether or not to allow these things to affect and impact us. We can't waste our tomorrows thinking about our yesterdays, and we shouldn't spend our precious 1440 minutes dwelling on the negative things that haven't happened yet, especially when there is so much beauty in the present moment.

As our time together in these pages comes to an end, I pray that when you close this book you will feel inspired, encouraged, and better equipped to take on the next 1440 minutes.

As the sun rises tomorrow, remind yourself, "I will make the most of every minute today!"

ACKNOWLEDGMENTS

Someone recently asked me, "What was the greatest day of your life?" I replied that I vividly recall three days that are equally great.

On a humid summer night some years back, I met the most incredible woman ever. I knew immediately my life would never be the same. One day of 1440 minutes is all it took to know that my life would be forever changed, because I knew I wanted to spend the rest of my minutes with her.

This led to the second equally great day, the one in which we decided we wanted to permanently transition from spending minutes together to spending our lifetimes together, changing the world.

The third equally world-changing day happened when Maxwell Ace came into our lives.

These three significant days blend together into one, the greatest day of my life.

Jennifer, not only is this book dedicated to you, so is the rest of my life! Love you and Max to the moon and back!

I also offer sincere thanks and gratitude to:

Alex Field and The Bindery agency: Your belief in me and vision for where we can take my message continues to blow my mind. I couldn't imagine this journey without you.

Keith Wall: Thank you for putting the pieces together!

Wade Olinger (The Connector): Love you, Woski!

Pastor Dino and Delyn Rizzo: There are no words to describe what you both mean to me! Love you both deeply!

Pastor Stovall and Kerri Weems: Thank you for believing and allowing us to carry the baton with you.

PC and Tammy Hodges: Your belief in me has pushed and propelled me further than you'll ever know.

Bishop Keith and Pastor Deborah Butler: Your guidance throughout this journey has pointed me in the right direction countless times.

Dr. John C. Maxwell: I never would have thought in a million years that God would grant me the opportunity to personally know you. Not only has it been a blessing to get to know you, but to have worked on a project together has been life-changing and extremely humbling. Thank you so much for your belief in me.

To every pastor and leader who granted me an opportunity to speak on your platform, thank you so much! I never take those moments for granted and cherish each one of those assignments.

To my CFC family, Celebration Church family, Arc family, and every one of my brothers and sisters who have dedicated their lives to building the kingdom of God and the body of Christ, I'm so grateful for you. My life is better because of your investment in me and my family.

To all of my uncles and aunties, thank you for everything!

To my friends (and you know who you are!), we are just getting started! More laughs, more memories, more life ahead.

Last but certainly not least, to *my family*!

To my mom, Brenda Timberlake: I am who I am because of you! Thank you for the eternal investment of love you have deposited in my life.

To my late father, Mack Timberlake Jr.: I pray I am making you proud up there, Big Guy!

Tmac and Momma MC: It's so evident that your love for me far outweighs the love you have for the other two kids. Thank you for showing me and vocalizing that favoritism.

Kimmy, Darrell, Nica, Dayana, Daila, Tim, Chris, Christianson, Carrigan, Quis, George, Majesty, Micah, and TT: Thank you all for loving me the way you do! Life is as sweet as it is because you all are my family!

NOTES

CHAPTER 2: EVERYDAY EXTRAORDINARY

1. Lexico, s.v. "ordinary," https://www.lexico.com/definition/ordinary.

CHAPTER 3: SEVEN DAYS OF SPLENDOR

1. Julia Guerra, "Why Can't I Remember What Day It Is? Science Says It's About More than Just Your Busy Schedule," Elite Daily, September 7, 2017, https://www.elitedaily.com/life/culture/much -trouble-remembering-day-week/2064207.

2. See "Life Is Not Measured . . . ," The Quote Investigator, December 17, 2013, https://quoteinvestigator.com/2013/12/17/breaths/.

3. For example, see Robert Provine, "The Science of Laughter," *Psychology Today*, November 1, 2000, https://www.psychologytoday .com/us/articles/200011/the-science-laughter, and David DiSalvo, "Six Science-Based Reasons Why Laughter Is the Best Medicine," *Forbes*, June 5, 2017, https://www.forbes.com/sites/daviddisalvo/2017 /06/05/six-science-based-reasons-why-laughter-is-the-best-medicine /?sh=56c477c57f04.

4. For more, see the website laughteryoga.org and Madan Kataria, *Laughter Yoga: Daily Practices for Health and Happiness* (New York: Penguin, 2020).

5. See "Practice Random Acts of Kindness . . . ," The Quote Investigator, November 22, 2017, https://quoteinvestigator.com /2017/11/22/kindness/.

6. Og Mandino, "Quotes: Quotable Quote," Goodreads, n.d., https://www.goodreads.com/quotes/733274-realise-that-true-happiness-lies-within-you-waste-no-time.

7. This is often attributed to the Greek philosopher Hermes Trismegistus; see Christopher Abel and William Hare, *Hermes Trismegistus: An Investigation of the Origin of the Hermetic Writings* (Sequim, WA: Holmes, 1997).

8. Yvette Nathalie Brown, "Mondays Don't Suck, Your Perception Does: How to Enjoy Every Day of the Week," ThePowerscope.com, August 12, 2019, https://www.thepowerscope.com/blackgirlblog/2019/8/12/mondays-dont-suck-your-perception-does-how-to-enjoy-every-day-of-the-week.

CHAPTER 4: VU DEJA

1. Jordan Gaines Lewis, "Why Do Some People Get Déjà Vu More Often than Others?" *Psychology Today,* October 13, 2015, https://www.psychologytoday.com/us/blog/brain-babble/201510/why-do-some-people-get-d-j-vu-more-often-others.

CHAPTER 5: "I'LL BE THE ONE"

1. The following is a paraphrase of Luke 17:11–17.

CHAPTER 7: KNOW WHERE YOU WANT TO GO

1. Leonard Ravenhill Quotes, https://www.leonard-ravenhill.com/quotes.

2. Jim Carrey, quoted in Leonard Kim, "I Think Everyone Should Get Rich and Famous," *Medium,* July 3, 2015, https://medium.com/@mrleonardkim/what-did-jim-carrey-actually-mean-ff98cea4b917.

CHAPTER 8: OUT OF CONTROL

1. For example, see Elliot D. Cohen, "The Fear of Losing Control," *Psychology Today,* May 22, 2011, https://www.psychologytoday.com/us/blog/what-would-aristotle-do/201105/the-fear-losing-control. Also see, Concordia University, "Fear of Losing Control and Its Role in

Anxiety Disorders: Study's Findings May Further Treatment of OCD, Panic Attacks, Social Phobia and More," Science Daily, December 13, 2017, www.sciencedaily.com/releases/2017/12/171213120047.htm.

CHAPTER 9: NOTHING CHANGES IF NOTHING CHANGES

1. Melissa G. Hunt, Rachel Marx, Courtney Lipson, and Jordyn Young, "No More FOMO: Limiting Social Media Decreases Loneliness and Depression," *Journal of Social and Clinical Psychology* 37, no. 10 (2018): 751–768, https://doi.org/10.1521/jscp.2018.37.10.751.

2. Eva Selhub, "Nutritional Psychiatry: Your Brain on Food," Harvard Health Blog, November 16, 2015, https://www.health.harvard.edu/blog/nutritional-psychiatry-your-brain-on-food-201511168626.

3. Franziska Spritzler, "6 Foods That Cause Inflammation," healthline.com, November 12, 2019, https://www.healthline.com/nutrition/6-foods-that-cause-inflammation#1.

4. Rudy Mawer, "6 Reasons Why High-Fructose Corn Syrup Is Bad for You," healthline.com, September 27, 2019, https://www.healthline.com/nutrition/why-high-fructose-corn-syrup-is-bad#1.

5. Mayo Clinic Staff, "Exercise: 7 Benefits of Regular Physical Activity," mayoclinic.org, May 11, 2019, https://www.mayoclinic.org/healthy-lifestyle/fitness/in-depth/exercise/art-20048389.

6. To better understand addictive behavior, see Gregory Jantz, *Healing the Scars of Addiction: Reclaiming Your Life and Moving into a Healthy Future* (Grand Rapids: Revell, 2018); Harry L. Haroutunian, *Being Sober: A Step-by-Step Plan for Getting to, Getting Through, and Living in Recovery* (Emmaus, PA: Rodale, 2013); and Al Mooney, *The Recovery Book: Answers to All Your Questions About Addiction and Alcoholism and Finding Health and Happiness in Sobriety* (New York: Workman, 2014).

CHAPTER 11: KEEP PERSPECTIVE THROUGH PLENTY

1. Carl Sagan, *Cosmos* (New York: Random House, 1980).

CHAPTER 12: TO MOVE BEYOND, LEAVE IT BEHIND

1. *Merriam-Webster Dictionary*, s.v. "victim," https://www.merriam
-webster.com/dictionary/victim.

CHAPTER 14: REST TO GIVE YOUR BEST

1. Jenna Fletcher, "Why Sleep Is Essential for Health," Medical News
Today, May 31, 2019, https://www.medicalnewstoday.com/articles
/325353#better-productivity-and-concentration.

CHAPTER 15: FACE YOUR FEAR

1. For more information, see "Chronic Stress Puts Your Health at Risk,"
Mayo Clinic, https://www.mayoclinic.org/healthy-lifestyle
/stress-management/in-depth/stress/art-20046037. See also Jerry
Kennard, "Why Stress Hormones Can Lead to Health Problems,"
Healthcentral.org, https://www.healthcentral.com/article/why-stress
-hormones-can-lead-to-health-problems.
2. Lexico, s.v. "courage," https://www.lexico.com/definition/courage.
3. Anita Wadhwani and Mariah Timms, "Sentenced to life in prison
at 16, Cyntoia Brown will walk free Aug. 7. Here's how it happened,"
Nashville Tennessean, July 30, 2019, https://www.tennessean.com/story
/news/2019/07/31/cyntioa-brown-released-from-prison-2019/1820393001/.
4. See "Gretzky's 4 Goals Rip Lindbergh & Co., 9–3," *Philadelphia
Inquirer*, February 9, 1983; "Blues Shut Out Red Wings," *New York
Times*, May 11, 1996, https://www.nytimes.com/1996/05/11/sports
/nhl-playoffs-blues-shut-out-red-wings.html.
5. To explore mindfulness meditation, check out the following apps:
calm.com, breethe.com, and headspace.com.

CHAPTER 16: TODAY, GIVE YOURSELF AWAY

1. Ed Mazza, "Starbucks 'Pay It Forward' Streak Lasts 11 Hours in
Florida," *Huffington Post*, August 21, 2014, https://www.huffpost
.com/entry/starbucks-pay-it-forward-streak_n_5697113.
2. Ira B. Wilson and George S. Schuler, "Make Me a Blessing," 1924,
renewed 1951.

CHAPTER 17: DESTINY IN A DAY

1. Lexico, s.v. "integrity," https://www.lexico.com/definition/integrity.
2. Martin Luther King Jr., *The Papers of Martin Luther King, Jr.,* Vol. 3: *The Birth of a New Age,* ed. Clayborne Carson (Los Angeles: University of California Press, 1997), 457.

CHAPTER 18: TRANSFORMED THROUGH TRANSPARENCY

1. Abigail Abrams, "Yes, Imposter Syndrome Is Real. Here's How to Deal with It," *Time,* June 20, 2018, https://time.com/5312483/how-to -deal-with-impostor-syndrome/.
2. Dr. Phil McGraw, "The Authenticity Litmus Test," drphil.com, July 13, 2005, https://www.drphil.com/advice/the-authenticity -litmus-test/.

CHAPTER 19: DEFEAT YOUR DOUBTS

1. Dan Nosowitz, "Daylight Savings Time Is Actually a Good Thing," *Popular Mechanics,* March 7, 2020, https://www.popularmechanics .com/science/environment/a18011/in-defense-of-daylight-saving-time/.

CHAPTER 20: THE POWER OF PERSPECTIVE

1. Alex Burmester, "How Do Our Brains Reconstruct the Visual World?" The Conversation, November 5, 2015, https://theconversation.com /how-do-our-brains-reconstruct-the-visual-world-49276.
2. Maria Konnikova, "Hamlet and the Power of Beliefs to Shape Reality," *Scientific American,* February 18, 2012, https://blogs.scientificamerican .com/literally-psyched/hamlet-and-the-power-of-beliefs-to-shape -reality/.

CHAPTER 23: MOTIVE MATTERS

1. Michael Blanding, "Lessons from the Lance Armstrong Cheating Scandal," *Forbes,* December 18, 2013, http://www.forbes.com/sites /hbsworkingknowledge/2013/12/18/lessons-from-the-lance-armstrong -cheating-scandal.

CHAPTER 24: STEP ONE

1. This statement is attributed to Chinese philosopher Lao Tzu and first appeared in his work *Tao Te Ching*, likely written between the fourth and sixth centuries.
2. See Bill Moyers's interview with Grisham, *Bill Moyers Journal*, http://www.pbs.org/moyers/journal/archives/grishamexcl_flash.html. See also Shaffer Todd, "John Grisham, 20 Years of Writing," Shaffer's Notebook, July 2, 2009, https://shaffersnotebook.wordpress.com/2009/07/02/john-grisham-20-years-of-writing/.

CHAPTER 26: MASTER OF ONE

1. This quote is attributed to Aristotle though some researchers dispute the origins. A different version appears in Aristotle's *Nicomachean Ethics*, book 2.
2. For more on this topic, see Charles Duhigg, *The Power of Habit: Why We Do What We Do in Life and Business* (New York: Random House, 2012) and the classic work by Stephen R. Covey, *The Seven Habits of Highly Effective People: Restoring the Character Ethic* (New York: Simon & Schuster, 1989).

CHAPTER 27: MIRACULOUS DISASTER

1. Alexander Harris, "U.S. Self-Storage Industry Statistics," SpareFoot, March 7, 2020, https://www.sparefoot.com/self-storage/news/1432-self-storage-industry-statistics/.
2. Joshua Fields Millburn and Ryan Nicodemus, "What Is Minimalism?" The Minimalists, n.d., https://www.theminimalists.com/minimalism/.
3. Henry David Thoreau, *The Portable Thoreau*, ed. Jeffrey S. Cramer (New York: Penguin, 2012), n.p.
4. Susan Krauss Witbourne, "5 Reasons to Clear the Clutter Out of Your Life," *Psychology Today*, May 13, 2017, https://www.psychologytoday.com/us/blog/fulfillment-any-age/201705/5-reasons-clear-the-clutter-out-your-life.

CHAPTER 28: FOOD INSPECTOR

1. See the story in Murray Teigh Bloom, "The Money Maker," *American Heritage* 35, no. 5 (August–September 1984), https://www.americanheritage.com/money-maker-0.

ABOUT THE AUTHOR

Tim Timberlake is the lead pastor of Celebration Church in Jacksonville, Florida, and Creedmoor, North Carolina. He is a gifted communicator and teacher who has the ability to communicate to people from all walks of life. His sense of humor, combined with his in-depth Bible teaching, gives the listener and reader the tools to transform their lives from the inside out. Tim is a graduate of the Pistis School of Ministry in Detroit, Michigan. He is an avid sports fan and a cultural thought leader.